CW00558183

LEICESTER TO NOTTINGHAM

also Syston Junction to Melton Mowbray

Vic Mitchell and Keith Smith

MP Middleton Press

Front cover: East Midlands Trains unit no. 222006 approaches Leicester station with a St Pancras working, on 23rd August 2014. Empty cement tanks from a Ketton-St Pancras circuit are on the right. The former EWS loco depot houses Class 56s and a Class 37. The depot was taken over in September 2013 by UK Rail Leasing Ltd, who purchased 15 surplus locos with the intention of hiring them to train operators. (P.D.Shannon)

Back cover: The 1947 Railway Clearing House map has our route via Trent. The more direct line is shown as LNER. This had been built by the Great Central Railway as a rival route and ceased to carry passengers in 1969. Partial revival has taken place more recently, in stages.

ACKNOWLEDGEMENTS

We are very grateful for the assistance received from many of those mentioned in the credits, also from A.J.Castledine, G.Croughton, G.Gartside, M.Greenwood, C.M.Howard, P.Jones, A.Morley, A.C.Mott, N.Langridge, A.Neale, D. and Dr S. Salter, E.Vaughan, T.Walsh, and in particular our always supportive families.

Published February 2018

ISBN 978 1 910356 15 9

© *Middleton Press, 2018*

Production Editor Deborah Esher
Typesetting and design Cassandra Morgan
Cover design Matthew Esher

Published by
        Middleton Press
        Easebourne Lane
        Midhurst
        West Sussex
        GU29 9AZ
Tel: 01730 813169
Email: info@middletonpress.co.uk
www.middletonpress.co.uk

Printed and bound by CPI Group (UK) Ltd, Croydon, CR0 4YY

CONTENTS

INDEX

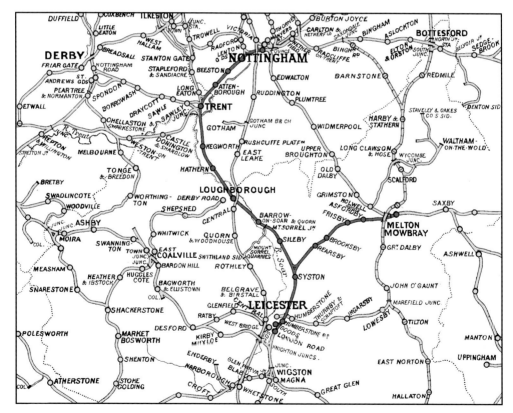

I. The routes of this album are bold on this extract from the Railway Clearing House 1947 map. The ownerships are shown on the back cover. Our journey north is via Syston and Trent.

GEOGRAPHICAL SETTING

The main line from Leicester to Trent Junction runs close to the north-flowing River Soar Navigation. This is part of the Grand Union Canal system and, near to Trent Junction, flows into the River Trent Navigation, part of the Trent and Mersey Canal system. The line from Syston Junction to Melton Mowbray follows the River Wreake which flows southwest, passing through Melton Mowbray, to join the Soar. In its upper reaches it is called the River Eye.

Both routes largely traverse red sandstones, but there is a small but notable exception west of Barrow-upon-Soar, where granite is produced in Mountsorrel Quarry. There are also some small outcrops of gypsum, used to produce plaster.

The lines to Loughborough and to Melton Mowbray are in Leicestershire. Trent and Long Eaton stations were built in Derbyshire. The remainder of the route runs through Nottinghamshire. The maps are to the scale of 25ins to 1 mile, with north at the top, unless otherwise indicated.

HISTORICAL BACKGROUND

The first main line to Leicester was that of the Midland Counties Railway southward from Trent Junction. It opened on 5th May 1840, and trains continued south to Rugby from 30th June 1840. Trent Junction was roughly halfway between Derby and Nottingham on the MCR's earliest line, which had come into use on 4th June 1839, and at Rugby the MCR met the London & Birmingham Railway which had opened in 1838. This formed the main line of communication between the East Midlands and the capital until 1857, when the route from Leicester to Bedford and Hitchin opened. The MCR became part of the Midland Railway in May 1844.

The branch to Melton Mowbray was opened by the MR on 1st September 1846, with three intermediate stations. It was extended east to Stamford in 1848. The direct route north to Nottingham was completed by the MR in 1879. The latter town had MR services to Lincoln from 1846 and the Great Central Railway links north and south from 1897, the latter running close to the main route in this album. The MR main line northwards from Trent Junction to Codnor Park had come into use in 1847. There are GCR details in caption 43 and its adjacent diagram.

The MR became a large part of the London, Midland and Scottish Railway in 1923 and this was a major constituent of the London Midland Region of British Railways under the Nationalisation scheme, in 1948.

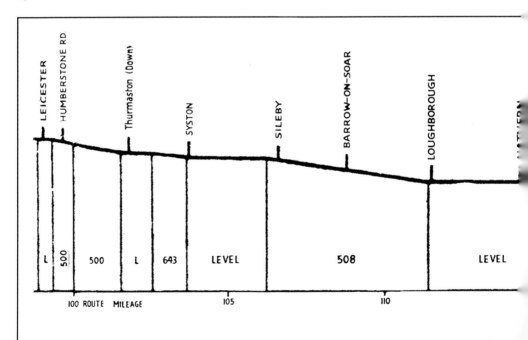

Following privatisation, main line services between Leicester and Nottingham, originating from St Pancras, were operated by Midland Mainline from 28th April 1996 until 10th November 2007. Local and regional services were run by Central Trains between 2nd March 1997 and 10th November 2007. These comprised services that originated from Coventry or Birmingham New Street and ran via Nuneaton and Leicester to Nottingham or Lincoln. This service was later split and the Coventry part withdrawn, operating as separate services between Birmingham New Street and Leicester and also between Leicester and Lincoln. On the northern part of the route, services to Nottingham, which originated from Cardiff Central or Birmingham New Street, operated via Derby. The latter service was operated under the 'Central Citylink' brand between 2003 and 2007.

From 11th November 2007, Midland Mainline services were amalgamated into the new East Midlands Trains franchise. The Central Trains franchise was split, with the Leicester to Lincoln services also becoming part of East Midlands Trains. Services from Birmingham New Street to Leicester and Cardiff or Birmingham New Street to Nottingham were merged into the new CrossCountry franchise on the same day.

On the Syston to Melton Mowbray route, services were operated between Birmingham New Street and Stansted Airport via Leicester by Central Trains from 2nd March 1997 until 10th November 2007, again under the 'Central Citylink' brand. On 11th November 2007 these were also transferred to the new CrossCountry franchise. Only a limited service was operated around the northern part of the triangle at Syston – one train a day ran to and from Derby to at least Corby, via Melton Mowbray and Oakham.

PASSENGER SERVICES

The table gives sample figures for trains running on at least five days per week. In the steam era, many of the journey opportunities shown below involved changing at Trent, which acted as the 'cross roads' for the district. Not shown are the stopping trains from the south, which terminated at Loughborough. In recent times, they have been hourly on weekdays.

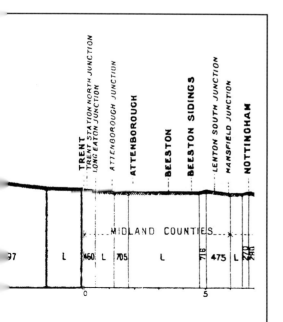

Leicester to Nottingham

	Fast		Stopping	
	Weekdays	Sundays	Weekdays	Sundays
1841	3	1	3	2
1872	6	2	8	2
1901	10	5	9	2
1931	9	3	11	3
1961	4	4	15	6
1995	19	6	8	0

By 2018, Syston northern triangle was only used by two up services from Nottingham to Norwich and one return late at night from Peterborough, weekdays only.

LONDON, LEICESTER, NOTTINGHAM, DERBY, SHEFFIELD, LEEDS, and SCOTLAND.

Miles	Down.	Week Days.																				
		mrn	mrn	mrn	mrn	mrn	mrn	mrn	mrn	mrn	mrn	mrn	mrn	mrn	mrn	mrn	mrn	mrn	mrn	mrn	mrn	mrn
	LONDON (St. Pancras) dep.	2 25													4 25							
49¾	**Bedford** (Midland Rd.) "														5 46							
53	**Oakley**																					
56¾	**Sharnbrook**																					
62¾	Irchester																					
76¾	**Northampton B** arr.																					
	412, 468, 470, 685 dep.																					
65	**Wellingboro' A** 470, 685,														6 13							
68½	**Finedon** [690																					
69½	Burton Latimer, for Isham																					
—	**677** CAMBRIDGE dep.																					
72	**Kettering** 677, 693	3 45													6 28							
75¼	**Glendon and Rushton C**																					
78	**Desborough & Rothwell D**																					
83	**Market Harboro** 468, 469,														6 48			7 3				
86¼	**East Langton** [895																	7 12				
88¾	**Kibworth**																	7 20				
91½	**Great Glen**												Saturdays only.					7 27				
95¼	**Wigston** (Magna)																	7 36				
99	**Leicester** (Lon. Road) arr.	4 19													7 12			7 44				
	688, 690 dep.	4 35										6 20	6 43	6 50	7 23		7 29	Stop		8 8		
99¾	Humberstone Road											6 23		6 53						8 11		
103¾	**Syston** 690											6 31	6 51	7 0			7 37			8 19		
106¾	Sileby F											6 38	6 57	7 6			7 43			8 25		
109	Barrow-on-Soar and Quorn											6 45	7 3	7 11			7 49			8 30		
111¼	**Loughboro'** (Mid.) G 844	4 58						Restaurant Cars, Sheffield to Glasgow. Through Express, Sheffield to Glasgow and Edinburgh.	Saturdays only. Through Express, Sheffield to Morecambe.	Saturdays only. Through Express, Heeley to L. & N. E. Line, see page 702.		6 52	7 10	7 16	7 40		8 5		Through Train to Halifax, via Thornhill (arrive Thornhill 10 12 mrn.), see pages 551 and 610.	8 35		
114¼	**Hathern**											7 0					8 11			Stop		
116¼	**Kegworth**											7 6	7 19				8 20					
119¾	**Trent** 694, 696 arr.						Saturdays only. Through Express, Heeley (dep. 7 35 mrn., see page 702) to Blackpool (T. Rd.) arr. 11 28 mrn.					7 14	7 27				8 30					
123¼	**Nottingham** 692, arr.											7 35					8 53					
	698, 700, 896 dep.		5 5									7 3			7§45	7 40	8 15					9 0
—	**Trent** dep.		5 18									7 22	7 28				8 35					
128¼	**Derby H** 656, 664 arr.	5 22	5 43									7 40			8 2	8 10	8 50					
147¾	**626** UTTOXETER arr.	8 10	8 10														9 46					
164¼	**626** STOKE-ON-TRENT "	8 55	8 55														1018					
165¾	**664** BUXTON "														9 27							
190	**664** MANCHESTER (Cen.) "	6 48	Stop												9 52		Stop				Saturdays only.	
189½	**664** " (Victoria) "																					
218¼	**664** LIVERPOOL (Central) "	8 35	mrn												1052							
—	**660** BRISTOL (Tem. Md.) dep.	Stop	1/10													1 10					5K12	
—	**660** BIRMINGHAM (New St) "		4/15													6 55	mrn				7 55	
—	**Derby** dep.	mrn	5/50								6 20	7 48				8 15	8 40				9 10	
146	Chesterfield I 697, 701	5 56	6/27			6 55					7 33	8 32	8 20				9 36				9 50	9 55
158¾	**Sheffield M** 664, 699, arr.	6 34	6/52			7 38					8 20	9 0				9 7	Stop	mrn		mrn	10 15	1023
	704, **904**, **911** dep.	6 40	7 0	7 3	7 13	8 3	7 45	7 55	8 10	8 15	8 25					9 12	Stop	9 17	9 22	9 25	10 20	
163¾	Rotherham (Masboro')		7 13	7 22	7 30		7 55	8 5	8 20	8 29	8 50					9 23		9 28		9 40	10 30	
165¾	**Parkgate and Rawmarsh**		7 19	7 28	7 35		8 0			8 36	8 55							9 36		9 46		
167¼	**Kilnhurst**	Via Chapeltown, see page 699.	7 25		7 40	Via Chapeltown, see page 699.	8 5			8 42	9 0							9 41				
168¾	Swinton 704, 721		7 30	7 34	7 44		8 10			8 47	9 4				Restaurant Car, Leicester to Buxton, except on Saturdays.			9 46		9 54		
204¼	**704** YORK arr.		Stop	9 5																		
285¾	**704** NEWCASTLE (Cen.) "		Stop	1110																		
170¾	Wath-on-Dearne				7 50						9 10							9 53				
173	**Darfield**				7 56						9 16							9 59				
176¾	**Cudworth** 727, 933				8 6		8 28		8 40		9 24					9 42	mrn	10 7	9 51		10 50	
181	**Barnsley P** 727, arr.	7 25			8 27	8 50			9 6		9 35					9 59	K					
	904, 918 dep.	Stop			7 53											9 16	9P52	9 16	9 16			
179¼	**Royston and Notton**	Stop			8 13													1014				
183	**Sandal and Walton**	mrn	mrn		8 21													1022				
186¾	**Normanton 550**, 945	6 21	7 42		8o37				8 56								1024	1030			11 10	
189¾	**550** WAKEFIELD (K'gate) arr.				8 51				9 19				Through Express to Blackpool (T. Rd.) arr. 12 19 aft.					1043	1052	d		
204	**550** HUDDERSFIELD "				9 39				1035									12 5	1035	d		
208¼	**550** HALIFAX "				9 48				1041							Restaurant Car to Bradford.		1145	1041	d		
211½	**945** YORK "				9 41													1223	r		12 5	
291¾	**945** NEWCASTLE (Cen.) "				12 9													2 52				
188	Altofts and Whitwood	6 24	7 45		8 41																	
190	Methley 616	6 30	7 51																			
191¾	**Woodlesford**	6 35	7 56		8 48																	
195¾	Hunslet [947, 948, 952	6 44	8 5																			
197¾	**Leeds Q** 706, 712, 934, arr.	6 50	8 12		9 0			8 50								1011	1042	1049			11 26	
216	**952** HARROGATE arr.	8 15			1010			1010								1133	1133	1155			12 58	
214	**712** ILKLEY 952 "	8*34			10 3			10 3									K	1237			12K37	
211½	**706** BRADFORD R "	7 42	8 55		10 3			9 18								1057		1145	1124	Z	11 55	
261¼	**706** CARNFORTH "															1253					2 45	
265¾	**706** MORECAMBE T "	11c25						1125	1145							1250		1W8			2 21	
310¾	**706** CARLISLE "							1138								1253					3 41	
426	**714 Glasgow** (St. Enoch) "							2A0								3 34						
408¾	**714 Edinbro'** (Wav.) "							2u0								3 55						

LONDON, LEICESTER, NOTTINGHAM, DERBY, MANCHESTER, LIVERPOOL, SHEFFIELD, LEEDS, SCOTLAND, &c.—Midland.

Week Days—*Continued from page 158.*

Down—Continued.	mrn	aft	mrn	mrn	mrn	mrn	mrn	aft	aft	aft	mrn	mrn	mrn	mrn	aft	mrn	aft	aft	non	aft	aft	aft	aft	aft	aft	aft	aft	aft	aft	aft	aft	aft
			1st & 3rd class Luncheon Cars, London to Manchester (Central). M'chester & L'pool Exp.	Goes forward at 11 25 mrn	First and Third Class Corridor Dining Express, London to Glasgow.		First and Third Class Corridor Dining Express, London to Edinbro'.							Manchester Special Express. Luncheon Carriages (1&3 class) from London to Manchester (Cen.).	Buxton and Liverpool Express.	North Express.—3rd class Luncheon Carriage, London to Nottingham.			Goes forward at 2 12 aft.				Manchester Express.	Scotch Express.—Corridor Dining Express London to Glasgow.— 1st and 3rd class.			Saturdays only.	Except Saturdays.	Saturdays only.	Satrdys only.	North Express.	
LONDON. Victoria (S.E.&C.) dp.				8 50									9 48	1047		1118			12 0		1221						1 2	1 2	1 2			
Ludgate Hill ″				9 24									1035	1121		1150			1232		1258						1 35	1 35	1 35			
Moorgate Street ¶ ″				9 48									1047	1135		12 3			1223		1 11						1 59	1 59	2 9	2 19		
ST. PANCRAS ¶ ″			10 5	1010	1030		1040						11 0	12 0	1210	1225			1 0				2 0	2 10			2 20	2 30	2 30		3 0	
Kentish Town ¶ ″				1014									11 5	12 4		1229			1 4		1 26						2 25	2 34	2 34	2 36		
Hendon ¶ ″				1026									1120						1 17		1 44						2 35		2 51	2 39		
Mill Hill													1125						1 23		1 50								2 56	3 6		
Elstree & Boreham Wood													1131						1 29		1y56								3 2	3 12		
Radlett													1137						1 35		2y2								3 8	3 18		
St. Albans 275, 343				1043								1125	1145				1 25		1 43		2y10						2 52	3 2	3 16			
Harpenden [Hoo			p									1134	1157				1 36		1 55		2y20						3 3	3 13	3 39			
Chiltern Green, for Luton																	1 42		2 1		Stop							r	r			
Luton 275			1045									1143	12 7				1 48		2 7							2 12	3 12	3 23	3 48		3 39	3 50
Leagrave												1151	Stop				Stop									2 19						3 56
Harlington, fr Toddington												1159														3 0	3 26					4 4
Flitwick												12 6														3 8	3 33					4 11
Ampthill												1211														3 13	3 38					4 16
Bedford 448, 503, 361			1111				1138				1145	1223			1 9											3 25	3 50					4 28
NORTHAMPTON 448 arr			1210												2 10																	
Oakley											1153																					4 40
Sharnbrook			G								12 1	1240														3 51						4 48
Irchester [362			G								1211		aft													4 1				aft		4 58
Wellingboro' 475, 456,											1216	1252	1 10									2 59				4 6				3 50	r	5 3
Northampton 344 ar											1237															5 40						5 40
353, 375, 374 dp											1145		1250	1250		1250				1250		2 40								3 30		Stop
Finedon											1225											3 6								3 57		
Isham & Burton Latimer						*					1229											3 10								4 2		aft
Kettering 490, 456	1043										1235	1 5	1 20	1 30		1 51				1 45		3 16	3 23			4 20				4 8	4.28	4 40
Glendon and Rushton											1245	Stop	Stop							Oo						Stop						4 49
Desborough and Rothwell	B b										1252									1 57												4 56
Market Harboro' 309,	11 1										1 0									2 5												5 4
East Langton [341, 361																				2 14												5 14
Kibworth	1113										1 12									2 20												5 20
Great Glen	Sat.										1 18									Sat.												5 26
Wigston	1123										1 25									2 30												5 36
BIRMINGHAM 494 arr.	1253										3 10				4 0					4 0			5 22									6 58
Leicester (Lndn Rd) arr.	1132		1217		1225						1 37			2 7	2 15					2 40		aft	4 0			aft			aft			5 47
494,491,476,504 dep.	1143		1222		1230				1245		1 45			2 12	2 21					2 55		3 40	4 5			4 10			4 35			Stop
Humberstone Road									1248											2 58						4 13						
Syston 491	Dd								1256		1 54									3 6						4 21						
Sileby									1 3		2 1															4 28						
Barrow-on-Soar & Quorn									1 9		2 7															4 34			4 49			
Loughborough 360	1158								1 14		2 12				r					3 17		3 55				4 39	aft		4 54			
Hathern									1 22											3 25						4 47	5 14					
Kegworth	Dd								1 28		2 22									3 30						Stop	5 20		5 4			
Trent 476, 484 to 489 arr.					Rr				1 35		2 29						aft			3 36		4 9					5 34		5 10			
Nottingham 484 arr.					1 21		1 6		1 55		2 46					2 55				3 57	aft	4 21		4 33					5 27		5 30	aft
487, 490, 304 d.			1222		Xx		1 11		1 26	2 5	2 22				2 22	3 0	3 7			3 25	3 32	4 7		4 37					5 6		5 35	6 10
Trent dep. for North (Local Trains 489)					Xx																											
dep. for Derby,									1 41	2 21	2 38						3 20			3 39	3 49	4 19					5 40		5 22			6 26
Sawley J. [M'chstr, &c.										2 25											3 53						5 44					
Sawley																					3 57											
Draycott [brook										2 29							Ii				4 0						5 48					
Borrowash, for Ock-										2 35											4 6						5 54					
Spondon [445										2 39											4 10						5 58					
Derby 476, 494 to 499	1226		1b0						1 55	2 46	2 51				3b0		3 33			3 52	4 20	4 32	4b42				6 7		5 35			6 39
476 BUXTON 476 arr.			2 22						Stop	Stop	Stop				4 10		Stop			5 28	Stop						Stop		Stop			Stop
476 MANCHESTER Central ″			2 30											4 15	5 0					5 45			6 20									
Victoria ″			3 2											4 25									6 22									

LONDON, LEICESTER, NOTTINGHAM, DERBY, SHEFFIELD, LEEDS and SCOTLAND

Week Days

Miles		No.	a.m	a.m	a.m	a.m	a.m	a.m	a.m	a.m	a.m	a.m	a.m	a.m	a.m	a.m	a.m	a.m	a.m	a.m	a.m	a.m	a.m	a.m	a.m	a.m	a.m	a.m	a.m	a.m	a.m	a.m	a.m	a.m	a.m	a.m
			RC London (St. Pancras) to Manchester Piccadilly	RC Bristol (T.M.) to Sheffield (Table 210)	Mondays only		RC Sheffield to Bradford					RC London to Manchester (Cen.)	RC Birmingham to Bradford (Table 210)			Saturdays only		Except Saturdays. MR & RC Birmingham (N. St.) to Newcastle (Table 210)	RC Nottingham to Hull (Paragon) arr 1222 pm	RC Sheffield to Bradford			Saturdays only	RC from Birmingham dep 8 25 am (Table 227)		THE PALATINE. RC and RC London to Manchester (Cen.)	RC Worcester dep 7 54 am to York (Table 210)		Except Saturdays	Saturdays only	RC Bristol (T.M.) to Bradford (Table 210)		THE WAVERLEY. RC and RC London to Edinburgh	RC Birmingham to Nottingham (Table 227)	Saturdays only	RC from Birmingham (Nuneaton Sats. only) (Table 227). RC Bristol to Sheffield (Table 210)
	LONDON (St. Pancras).. dep	1	1 0		1 30							4 25												6C40		7 55						8 10	9 10			
20	St. Albans (City) ″	2																						7C16		7H42						8Z23				
30¼	Luton (Midland Road).. ″	3										5 8												7C31		8H29						8 48				
49¾	Bedford (Midland Rd.).. ″	4										5 37												8 21								9 11				
65	Wellingboro' A arr	5										6 1												8 43		9 6						9 33				
78¾	Northampton (Castle) arr	6										7N16												9 9								10 21				
	dep	7																				7 0				8 7										
—	Wellingboro' A dep	8										6 6								7 2		7 40		Stop		9 7						9 35				
72	Kettering arr	9										6 16								7 13		7 51										9 45				
	dep	10										6 21					6 50			7 15		7 54			8 45							9 47				
78	Desborough & Rothwell B.	11															7 4			7 27		8 6			8 56											
83	Market Harborough	12										6 41					7†15			7 37		8†17			9 6							10 4				
86¼	East Langton	13															7 21			7 45		8 23			9 12											
89	Kibworth	14															7 28			7 51		8 30			9 18											
95¼	Wigston (Magna)	15															7 38			8 1		8 40														
99	Leicester (London Rd) arr	16	3 1		3 23							7 1					7 46			8 9		8 48		a.m	9 33	9 44						10 25				
	dep	17	3 8		3 33					6 10	6 50	7 10				7 38		8 0			8 35			9 30		9 48		9 55				10 32		1040		1140
99¾	Humberstone Road	18								6 12	6 52					7 40	Stop	8 2		Stop		Stop												1042		1142
103¾	Syston	19								6 21	6 58					7 46		8 9			8 41			9 36				10 1						1048		1148
105¾	Sileby	20								6 28	7 3					7 51		8 15			8 46			9 41										1053		1153
109	Barrow-on-Soar and Quorn	21								6 34	7 8					7 56		8 21			8 51			9 46										1058		1158
111½	Loughborough (Mid.)	22								6o30	7 13	7 27				8 1		8 28			8 56			9 51				1012				10 47		11 3		12 3
116¼	Kegworth	23								7 0						8 8					9 2							1019						11 9		12 9
119¾	Trent arr	24								7 8	Stop					8 15		Stop			9 8			10 1				1025						1116		1218
123½	Nottingham (Mid.) arr	25			4 13					7 31	a.m					8 29	a.m				9 23	a.m		1015				1039				11 10	1116	1131		1231
	dep	26							6 13		7 10			7 35	8 0		8 14		8 57		9 0	9 10	9 40				1010	1040					1121	1110	1150	
—	Trent dep	27			Stop						7 23					Stop	8 27				9 17	9 23	9 52				1023	1050						1123	12 2	Stop
128½	Derby (Midland) arr	28	3 48								7 47	7 55		8 6			8 50				9 34	9 48	1010			1021	1048	1111						1147	1225	
164¼	128 STOKE-ON-TRENT arr	29										9 13		9 13			1013					1113						1213						1713		
165¼	211 BUXTON ″	30									Stop	9 21		9 21							1051					1130	Stop									
190	211 MANCHESTER (Cen.)... ″	31	5A25									9 46		9 46							1125					1154										
218½	211 LIVERPOOL (Central). ″	32	7P35									10 46		1046				a.m			1215					1 15	a.m									a.m
—	Derby (Midland) dep	33		5 47				6 30					7 58					9 0									1030				11 14					1156
146½	Chesterfield (Midland)	34	Stop	6 23			7r 0	7 24	8o 2				8 42		9 10			9 32	9 38		Stop						11 0				11 48		12 9			
158¼	Sheffield (Mid) arr	35		6 46	a.m		7r30	8 0	8 36		a.m		9 0		9 35	a.m		9 51	9 56	a.m	a.m						1128				12 9		1227			1247
	dep	36			7 6	7 10	7 44				8 40		9 9			9 40		10 0	10 5	10 10	11 6						1134		1140	1138	12 15		1233			
174¾	BARNSLEY arr	37		7 27				8 43	9 20						1028				11 28								1228				12S54		1 28			1 28
164	Rotherham (Masboro')	38			7 15	7 24	7 54				8 53		9 20			9 52		1011	10 15	10 21	1115						1146		1150	1151	12 26					
166	Parkgate and Rawmarsh	39		Stop	7 19	7 29					8 57					9 57													1155	1156						
167¾	Kilnhurst (West)	40			7 23						9 1								10S22										1159	12 1						
169	Swinton (Town)	41			7 26	7 35					9 5					10 4			10S25	10 32	1123								12 2	12 5						
205	YORK arr	42			8 32											11 5		1113	12d10		1216						1253									
285½	NEWCASTLE ″	43			10 38													1 4			2 9						3 33									
171	Wath (North)	44				7 42					9 11																		12 9	1212						
173¾	Darfield	45	a.m	a.m		7 51					9 18																		1215	1220						
177	Cudworth	46	6 21	7 23		8 1					9 27		9 50																1225	1229						
179¾	Royston and Notton	47	6 27	7 29		8 7														10 57									1230	1235						
183¾	Walton	48	6 37	7 39		8 17																							1238	1245						
187	Normanton	49	6 45	7 47		8 26	8 42						10 10							11 12									1218	[illegible]	1 13					
190	142 WAKEFIELD (K'gate).. arr	50		8 7			8 57						10 52							11 55									1 58	1 58	1 58					
211½	YORK ″	51	7 47																	12 33									1 41	1 41						
292	NEWCASTLE ″	52	1038																	3 33									4 17	4 17						
188¼	Altofts and Whitwood	53	6 50	7 52		8 31																							1253	1258						
191¾	Woodlesford	54	6 57	7 59		8 38																														
196	Hunslet	55																																		
198	Leeds (City) arr	56	7 7	8 10		8 49	8 57						10 27							11 30									1 6	1 13	1 32		1 43			
216½	HARROGATE arr	57	8 31	9K26			10 0						11 50							12K26											2K31		3K26			
214½	ILKLEY ″	58	8 55				9 53						11 51							12 57									1 53				2 51			
211½	BRADFORD (For. Sq.). ″	59	8 15	9 23			9 33						11 6							12 5											2 5		2 23			
311	209 CARLISLE ″	60											1 13																				4 14			
426	209 Glasgow (St. Enoch). ″	61											3 55																							
408½	209 Edinburgh (Wav.).... ″	62											4 34																				6 56			

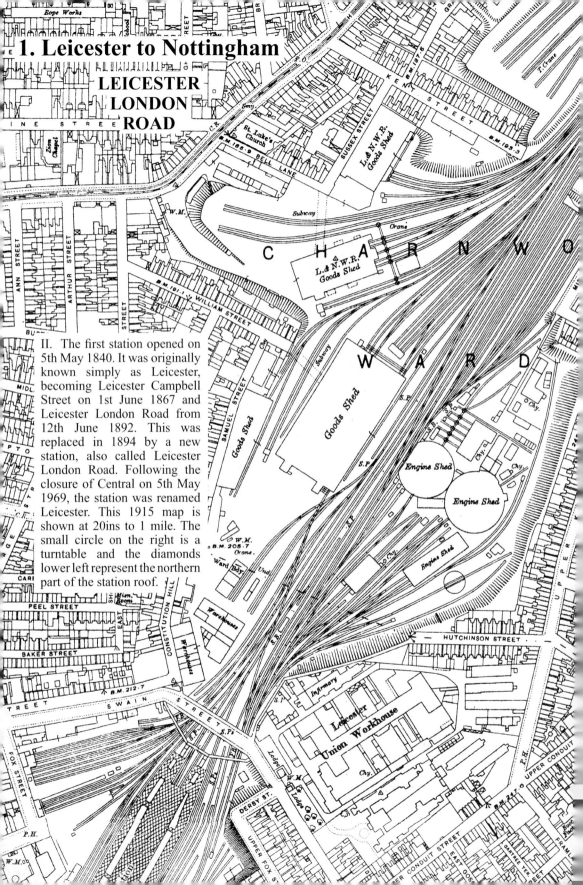

1. Leicester to Nottingham

LEICESTER LONDON ROAD

II. The first station opened on 5th May 1840. It was originally known simply as Leicester, becoming Leicester Campbell Street on 1st June 1867 and Leicester London Road from 12th June 1892. This was replaced in 1894 by a new station, also called Leicester London Road. Following the closure of Central on 5th May 1969, the station was renamed Leicester. This 1915 map is shown at 20ins to 1 mile. The small circle on the right is a turntable and the diamonds lower left represent the northern part of the station roof.

1. Cars from the 1930s are to be seen on this postcard view of the splendid 1894 structure. The tram tracks were in use from 1904 until 1949. Features from the pre-war period include a cream and red telephone box and cigarette promotion: Players Please. (J.Alsop coll.)

2. The important aspect of the station is seen after the Nazi bombing and the sidings are almost full. This is a southward panorama from Swain Street bridge. With the advent of power signalling in 1986, the signal box and the crossovers disappeared, and the tracks approaching the station were relaid to allow trains from any direction to enter or leave any platform. Leicester was granted city status in 1919 and gained a cathedral eight years later. (R.Humm coll.)

3. Mailbags abound on 20th June 1964, as class 9F 2-10-0 no. 92102 runs through with an up mixed freight train. Postal trains ceased to call here in 1996. (E.Wilmshurst)

WEST SIGNAL BOX

4. West Box was in use from 13th August 1893 until 28th June 1970. It had two 12-lever frames. East Box came into action and closed on the same dates. It housed a 12 and an 18-lever frame. It had a predecessor for at least 15 years. (R.J.Essery coll.)

LEICESTER

5.   The roof was demolished shortly after this photo of no. 45126 was taken on 5th July 1975. It was hauling the 17.25 from St. Pancras to Derby. The roof had been badly damaged during the bombing of World War II and the remaining glass was removed. (T.Heavyside)

6.   We are looking at the west side of the station and centre are Campbell Street sidings, which were used mainly for postal traffic. The first station had been in this area. On the right are Fox Street sidings, which include an end-loading dock used for wheeled equipment. Seen on 18th August 1979 is no. 47330 arriving from St Pancras and no. 08609 shunting a van. Two island platforms with four through roads were available from 1975. (T.Heavyside)

LEICESTER,—

Park Hotel,

Family & Commercial,

125, LONDON ROAD.

Three minutes from Midland Station.
Turn to the left.

TERMS MODERATE.

The Misses BAKER.

LEICESTER.—**"Crescent" Commercial Hotel,**
38, Regent Road (corner of King Street). Five minutes from Midland Station *via* Waterloo and
Regent Road. A Select Hotel for Commercial Gentlemen only (no accommodation for ladies)
Liberal Table. Plain Tea or Breakfast 1/-. Tea, Bed and Breakfast, including fish or
meat 4/6. No charge for attendance

Proprietress, Mrs. HENRY EDWARD BEER.

LEICESTER.—

"CARISBROOKE,"

Corner of

Stanley Road, Stoneygate.

Tea, Bed and Breakfast, 5/6 per night.

Two minutes from Victoria Park.   Trams pass the doors.

Nat. Telephone, 571 and 4663.

ALSO

"GABLES," 118, London Road,

Private and Commercial Hotel,

Tea, Bed and Breakfast, 4/6 per night.

LEICESTER.—**WAVERLEY COMMERCIAL HOTEL,**
Town Hall Lane (nr. Clock Tower.) The most central position
for Commercial Gentlemen. Excellent Table. Only prime English
Meat used. Comfortable and quiet. Tea, Bed and Breakfast, 4/6.
Baths (h. & c.) Special Week-end Terms.

F. FRANKEN, Proprietor,
Phone 4411.   (Late of Midland Hotel, Manchester,
Great Northern Hotel, Leeds.)

LEICESTER.—**The County Hotel,** Com-
mercial Unlicensed. Under personal Management. London Road,
corner of East Street ; nearly opposite Midland Station.
National Telephone 4664.   L. A. FOXON, Proprietress.

LEICESTER.—

The EDINBURGH Temperance Hotel,

18, KING STREET (corner of New Walk). Central. Comfortable
Commercial, Smoke, and Bedrooms.   THE MISSES WADDINGTON.

LEICESTER.—   **"Stop Here!"**

The CITY TEMPERANCE HOTEL,

Tariff from 4/6.   **157, London Road.**

Five minutes from Midland Station. Trams to door. Turn to the left. Commercial
and Smoke Room. Highly commended. Try it!   Mrs. and Miss PERRY.

LEICESTER.—**Argentine House,** 17, Highfield Street, 4 minutes
above Midland Station, London Road, Tea, Bed and Breakfast, 4/6 ; Bed and Breakfast (odd
night) from 3/6 ; Full-day Fare, 5/6. No charge for attendance Boots meets Trains Highly
recommended Commercial Gentlemen. *Ici on parle Francais.* Proprietress, Mrs. SHIRLEY.

GOOD ✝ LINES.

Thomas Cook ran the world's first excursion train on 5th July 1841. He organised one from Leicester to a Temperance meeting in Loughborough. These notices are taken from *Good Lines*, the monthly journal of the Temperance Society, dated January 1911.

7.   The east end of the porte-cochère was dedicated to taxis and this part was carefully adapted for pedestrians and less mobile passengers. A car park had dominated the area earlier. This is the peaceful scene on 21st July 2015. (V.Mitchell)

8.   On 31st March 2016, Meridian no. 222102 departs from platform 2 with the 10.29 St Pancras-Nottingham service. It is passing under the footbridge linking the platforms with the station car park. A 1st class lounge was provided at the far end of the left platform in 2000. (A.C.Hartless)

9.   Seen on 18th September 1909 is 4-4-0 no. 702 arriving with the 1.50pm from Manchester. The train included portions from Liverpool and Blackburn. It is passing North Box, which had 65 levers and was open from about 1890 to 1st June 1986. The box to the right of it is detailed in the next picture and the later sheds are shown in picture 11. They are on maps II and III. (R.J.Essery coll.)

10.   The Engine Shed Sidings signal box just worked the sidings and had 24 levers. It functioned from 18th September 1898 until 29th December 1968. Class 8F 2-8-0 no. 48169 is running on the up goods line on 11th June 1960. The gas works here and at Nottingham were not on the route of this volume and so are detailed in other Leicester albums. Intermediate gas works traffic is mentioned in a few captions herein. (M.J.Stretton coll.)

11.   The two round houses were replaced with this shed. It contained a central turntable from which 32 roads radiated. This took place in 1952, along with the erection of the coaling tower, left. On the right is the repair shed. The code was 15C in 1948-63 and 15A until closure in 1966. There were 80 engines based here in 1950, but only 24 in 1959. (M.J.Stretton)

12.   This is the scene on 19th April 1975, after the main shed had been demolished. Diesel types 25, 45 and 08 are evident and centre is the small shelter over the fuel filling pumps. (F.Hornby)

HUMBERSTONE ROAD

HUMBERSTONE ROAD

LEICESTER

HUMBERSTONE Rᴰ JUNCTION S.B. 100ᴹ16ᶜ
RICHARDS FOUNDRY SIDING 100ᴹ25ᶜ
L. AND N. E. G.N. SECTION
GREAT NORTHERN BRIDGE Nᴼ 11: 100ᴹ15ᶜ
HUMBERSTONE ROAD SIDINGS S.B. 100ᴹ10ᶜ
JUNCTIONS 100ᴹ15ᶜ
TO THANET
TO MAREFIELD

GOODS PASSᴳ (BELGRAVE ROAD) (G.N.)

LEICESTER CO-OPERATIVE SOCIETY'S FLOUR MILL
JUNCTION 99ᴹ79ᶜ
END OF 2ᴺᴰ DOWN GOODS LINE 99ᴹ78ᶜ
HUMBERSTONE ROAD STATION WHARF 99ᴹ76ᶜ
Long Eaton

HUMBERSTONE ROAD COAL DEPÔT
ALSO LEICESTER CORPᴺ SYSTON Sᵀ DEPÔT
100ᴹ50ᶜ

HUMBERSTONE ROAD 99ᴹ67ᶜ
NEDHAM Sᵀ WHARF JUNCTION 99ᴹ64ᶜ
JUNCTION 99ᴹ63ᶜ
GIMSON'S SIDING 99ᴹ60ᶜ

NEDHAM STREET WHARF 100ᴹ4ᶜ
JUNCTION 99ᴹ55ᶜ
BELL LANE S.B 99ᴹ49ᶜ

L.M.& S. GOODS STATION 99ᴹ72ᶜ (LNW)
TAYLOR & HUBBARD'S SIDING 99ᴹ44ᶜ
JUNCTION 99ᴹ42ᶜ

L.M.& S. GOODS STATION 99ᴹ28ᶜ (MID.)
ENGINE SHED SIDINGS S.B. 99ᴹ29ᶜ
ENGINE SHEDS 99ᴹ29ᶜ
STATION NORTH S.B & ENGINE SHED JUNCTION 99ᴹ19ᶜ

PASSENGER STATION 99ᴹ6ᶜ
STATION EAST & WEST S.Bs 99ᴹ7ᶜ

LONDON ROAD JUNCTION S.B. 98ᴹ74ᶜ

LONDON ROAD JUNCTION

Sheffield
Chesterfield
Derby
Nottingham
Beeston
East Midlands Parkway
Loughborough
Corby
Leicester
Market Harborough
Kettering
Wellingborough
Bedford
Luton
Luton Airport Parkway
London St Pancras

III. Bell Lane Signal Box can be found near the centre of the left diagram. It opened on 22nd October 1893 and had a 43-lever frame. A panel was added in 1979, to control a larger area. It closed on 29th June 1986. This 1923 diagram clarifies the complex series of goods facilities. The Needham Street sidings were the last to close (in 1983). Four of them were subsequently used by the scrap firm, Vic Berry Co. Its largest site was near Central station and the main activity was dismantling railway stock. It ran from 1973 to 1991. The ex-GNR line is shown across the top of the map, ending at Belgrave Road. It is illustrated in pictures 111 to 120 in our *Market Harborough to Newark* album. Caption 110 has details of the connection between the routes. The coal depot shown became Hercock Simpson's oil sidings. The right diagram is of East Midlands Trains InterCity services showing the 2018 service pattern each hour.

13. Creeping on the up freight line in about 1959 is class 8F 2-8-0 no. 48401 with a long goods train. This engine type was introduced in 1935 by the LMS. The words on the skyline are COOPERATIVE MILL. The business is now better known for grocery retailing. (Milepost 92½)

IV. At 14ins to 1 mile is the 1915 edition, which has the station shown above the tram tracks on the left. To the left of it is shown a 'Wharf', usually known as a 'Yard'. Running across the top of the map is the 1882 GNR line to its Leicester Belgrave Road terminus, which was beyond the left border.

14. The 4.25pm Manchester Central to St Pancras is seen behind 4-6-2 no. 70017 *Arrow* on 28th May 1960. *Britannia* was better known, as the first in the class in 1951. Many lamps were not replaced after the blackout of WWII. The yard had a 10-ton capacity crane, while Needham Street Wharf had one rated at 25tons. (H.Gamble/M.J.Stretton)

For other views of this area, see *Coventry to Leicester, Leicester to Burton*, *Market Harborough to Newark*, *Wellingborough to Leicester* **and** *Rugby to Loughborough.*

15. Also seen on 28th May 1960 is class 4F 0-6-0 no. 44509 with the 6.35pm Leicester London Road to Peterborough service. On the east side of the line were sidings for a corn mill, a timber yard and two engineering works. Passenger service was provided here from 1st July 1875 to 4th March 1968. (H.Gamble/M.J.Stretton)

16. Humberstone Road Junction Box opened on 30th December 1888 and was given a new 36-lever frame in 1902. Pictured in May 1973, closure came on 29th September 1979. The station was rebuilt on the Battlefield Steam Railway, at Shenton; see our *Nuneaton to Loughborough* album, picture 12. It was listed Grade II and was sold to the County Council for £1 plus VAT, for preservation. (M.A.King/R.Humm)

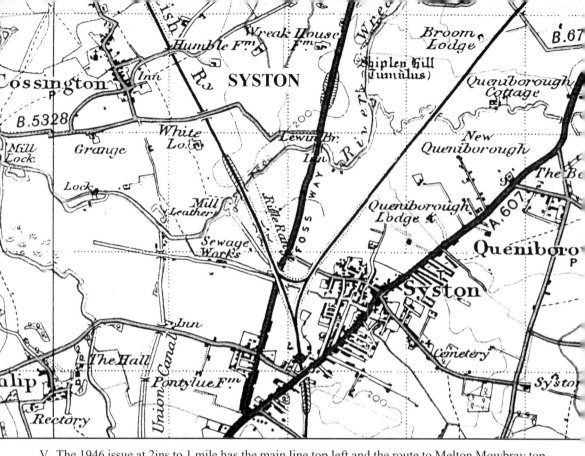

V. The 1946 issue at 2ins to 1 mile has the main line top left and the route to Melton Mowbray top right. The Grand Union Canal is lower left; boats turned left on reaching the River Wreake. The Foss Way was of Roman origin and it became the A46 in 1919. Top left is Cossington, which had a station called 'Cossington Gate' from 1st December 1845 until 29th September 1873. 'Gate' refers to part of a level crossing, in use until that year, when quadrupling brought the provision of a bridge and withdrawal of local staff. The west to east curve was opened in 1854. See pictures 96 and 97.

17. The prospective passenger's perspective was recorded on an early postcard, with the 'taxis' of the day awaiting. The local population was 2930 in 1901, rising to 6455 by 1961. The fine building was carefully dismantled in 2006 and rebuilt at the Midland Railway Centre at Butterley. (P.Laming coll.)

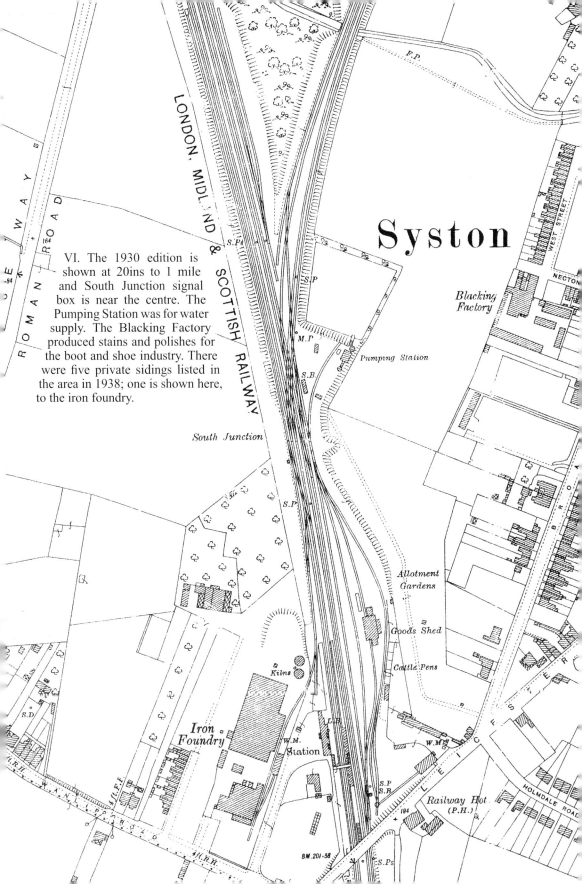

VI. The 1930 edition is shown at 20ins to 1 mile and South Junction signal box is near the centre. The Pumping Station was for water supply. The Blacking Factory produced stains and polishes for the boot and shoe industry. There were five private sidings listed in the area in 1938; one is shown here, to the iron foundry.

Syston

Blacking
Factory

Pumping Station

M.P

S.B

South Junction

S.P

Allotment
Gardens

Goods Shed

Cattle Pens

Kilns

Iron
Foundry

W.M.
Station

Railway Hotel
(P.H.)

LONDON, MIDLAND & SCOTTISH RAILWAY

ROMAN ROAD

BM.201·58

18. This card was post-marked 1912 and this fine panorama reveals that the centre tracks did not serve passengers. The goods yard was in use until 4th March 1968 and, unusually, passenger service was withdrawn the same day. White shirts were popular with the track gang, which is near the ground frame. The Syston & Thurmaston Gas Co. had no siding. They took only 900 tons of coal in 1900, rising to 2000 by 1928. The business was purchased by Leicester Gas Department. (P.Laming coll.)

19. The 5.32pm from Peterborough to Leicester is behind 'Patriot' class 4-6-0 no. 45503 *The Royal Leicestershire Regiment* on 17th May 1960. We have the opportunity to study the signalling of all four tracks south of South Junction. (M.J.Stretton coll.)

20. Carrying the appropriate Trainload Construction livery, no. 56055 passes Syston with the daily Mountsorrel-Radlett stone train on 2nd September 1989. At that time the Blue Circle cement terminal, in the former station goods yard, was still standing but no longer in use. It had closed on 7th October 1987. South Junction Box had been to the right of the tail of the train. (P.D.Shannon)

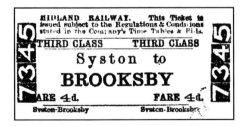

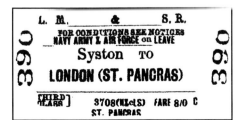

21. The station was reopened on 30th May 1994 by providing one 3-car platform near the edge of the old goods yard site, adjacent to the bidirectional single track from East Junction to Leicester. This is a special train on opening day. Homes were built on much of the disused railway land. (M.J.Stretton)

22. The 11.19 Tinsley to Bardon Hill empty stone train heads south behind Freightliner Heavy Haul no. 66604 on the 12th November 2013. The train is crossing from the slow line to the fast. This flow was later worked by GB Railfreight. (R.Geach)

23. We proceed north to South Junction in the 1920s or early 1930s. The locos are nos 2384 and 3452. The 37-lever box was in use from 24th July 1910 to 11th April 1987. (R.J.Essery coll.)

24. We can now have a close examination of South Junction and its 57-lever box in August 1985. It was opened on 26th November 1911 and worked until 11th April 1987. All the up signals are evident. (R.J.Stewart-Smith)

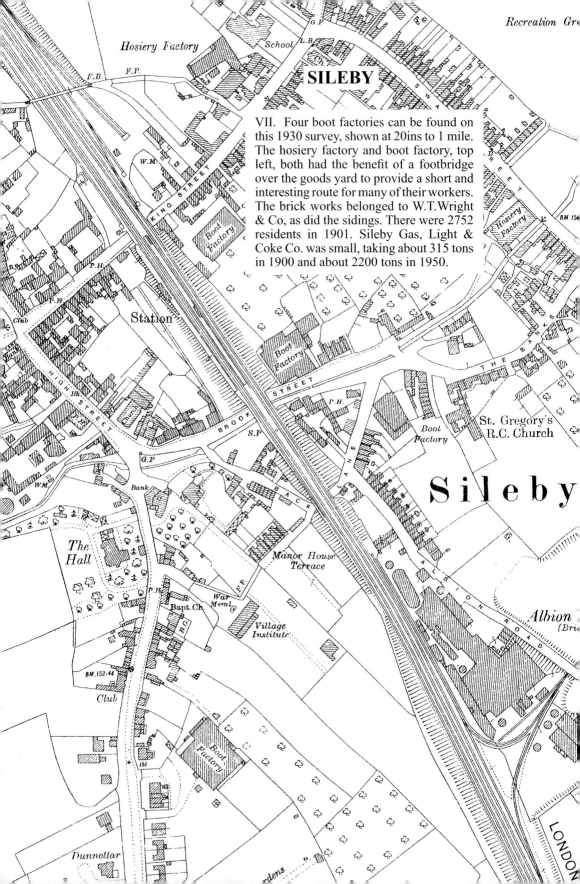

Recreation Gr

SILEBY

VII. Four boot factories can be found on this 1930 survey, shown at 20ins to 1 mile. The hosiery factory and boot factory, top left, both had the benefit of a footbridge over the goods yard to provide a short and interesting route for many of their workers. The brick works belonged to W.T. Wright & Co, as did the sidings. There were 2752 residents in 1901. Sileby Gas, Light & Coke Co. was small, taking about 315 tons in 1900 and about 2200 tons in 1950.

Hosiery Factory

School

L.B.

F.B.

F.P.

KING STREET

W.M.

Boot Factory

Hosiery Factory

BM 15

P.H.

Station

HIGH STREET

BK

Boot Factory

STREET

BROOK

S.P.

P.H.

THE BANKS

Boot Factory

St. Gregory's R.C. Church

G.P

Bank

W.M.

BACK

Sileby

The Hall

P.H.

Bapt. Ch.

B.G.

War Mem

Manor House Terrace

Village Institute

P.P.

JANE

ALBION ROAD

Albion (Bri

BM.152·44

Club

Boot Factory

151

Dunnottar

rdens

LONDON

25. This view south is from April 1904. The entire range of features had been created on an embankment. The barrows were for parcels traffic, but it was cheaper to send them by goods train. There was a shed in the yard to receive them, but all activity there ceased on 6th April 1964. Milk churns ceased to appear in the 1930s. (R.J.Essery coll.)

26. We now look north on the same occasion and find the goods yard centre. Quadrupling took place in 1906 and the fence was removed. On the left is the path up from King Street. The map shows that it was later lengthened and thus made less steep. The lamps used gas. (R.J.Essery coll.)

27.   A day excursion train from Leicester to Blackpool speeds through on 17th August 1962, hauled by 'Jubilee' class 4-6-0 no. 45614 *Leeward Islands*. All passenger trains ceased to call from 4th March 1968. The nearest door was for the benefit of Gentlemen and for those who had to fill the nearby fire buckets. (M.J.Stretton coll.)

28.   The 1898 signal box sets the scene for no. 45141 heading south with the 12.19 Derby-St Pancras on 16th April 1983. The box and semaphores were replaced by multiple aspect signalling on 11th April 1987. The middle post on the up bracket signal shows that there was once a crossover here. The box opened on 18th December 1898 and had a 29-lever frame. (P.D.Shannon)

29. A view from the footbridge just north of Sileby, on 13th November 2013, has no. D1015 *Western Champion* working the 11.21 Wellingborough to Mountsorrel empty stone service on the down fast line. On the left can be seen the short platforms, together with one of the slopes down to the road. On Monday to Saturdays, there was an hourly service southbound to Leicester and northbound to Nottingham, continuing onwards to Lincoln Central. There was no Sunday service. (R.Geach)

30. The station reopened on 30th May 1994, as at Syston, but there were no trains linking them. Specials called at both stations on 28th May, as part of the creation of the 'Ivanhoe Line'. Mobile phones are in action as no. 156406 approaches with the 11.40 Lincoln-Leicester service on 26th August 2017. As at Barrow-upon-Soar, the original station here had its platforms on the other two tracks. There were around 123,000 passengers in 2016. (P.D.Shannon)

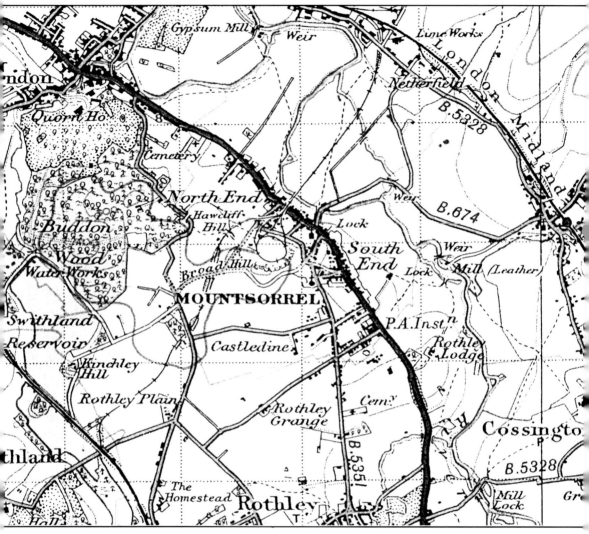

VIII. Sileby station is on the right of this 1946 map, which is shown at 2ins to 1 mile. The sidings to Barrow Lime Works are near the top and close to the word 'London'. The track around the granite quarry is shown as a circle and diverging from it is the 1896 line linking it with the GCR. This is shown diagonally across the lower left corner. Marked P.A.Institution is the 1930 successor to the Work House. The locks are on the River Soar on which the quarry output was conveyed in the days of road setts and until 1860, when a bridge over it was built for the quarry line. Setts were made until 1936 and kerbs until 1940. The quarry was extended into Buddon Wood in the 1970s and 7.8m tons were created per annum by 1989 and over 150 were employed. The first train ran on the revived GCR from Rothley on 8th September 1975 and the quarry connection can be seen in the *Rugby to Loughborough* Middleton Press album, in pictures 100-102. The GCR quarry line was gradually relaid and a museum, plus a heritage centre, were established. The Prince of Wales undertook a ceremonial opening on 25th January 2016 and rode on class 3F 0-6-0T no. 47406, thus creating the shortest royal train ever. The formal opening was of the 1¾ mile-long line from Swithland Sidings to the new station at the quarry. The intermediate one was at Nunckley Hill. The formal opening was on 24th October 2015. The line to the quarry from the north was replaced by a conveyor belt in 1977.

31. A view from the Redland period reveals the ease of loading. The site has one of the world's largest rock crushers. The quarry itself covers 167 acres and drops to 120m below sea level. The pink stone is used extensively for road surfacing after asphalt coating and in concrete. Around 1m tons went annually as track ballast. It took less than two hours to load 1350 tons into a 36-wagon train. (R.Humm coll.)

IX. The 2013 diagram shows the extensive facilities, with LS indicating Locomotive Shed and SN, Shunt Neck. Dashes across the tracks indicate a footpath crossing. The lines became private sidings on 24th October 2015. The names applied were Redland from 1959, Lafarge from 1997 and Tarmac from 2015. Conveyor belts extended for over 1½ miles to the sidings. (©TRACKmaps)

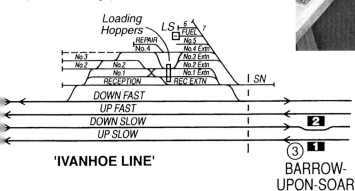

'IVANHOE LINE'

BARROW-UPON-SOAR

↓ 32. Loading is under way on 19th April 2011. Care has to be taken to load each wagon evenly. If too much granite is concentrated over one bogie, then it affects the stability of the wagon on the main line and in an extreme case could cause a derailment. The control room is just visible on the left. (P.D.Shannon)

33. No. 66712 draws its train of 'Mussel' ballast wagons under the loader on the same day. It will form the 10.25 departure to Eastleigh. The 'Mussels' were built by Greenbrier in Poland in 2009 and have a payload capacity of 77.3 tonnes, which is greater than any other design of ballast wagon. About 70% of the total output from Mountsorrel leaves the site by rail, which means up to eight departures in a typical 24-hour period. (P.D.Shannon)

34. We can enjoy now an overview of the Lafarge loading facilities on the same day. The wagons in the foreground are the latest 'Mussel' ballast wagons and are being loaded with granite ballast, while on the right a short rake of self-discharge wagons undergoes servicing. The entire fleet of self-discharge wagons was taken out of service in November 2016, following an accident. Shunting was undertaken by an Italian-built Zephir tractor, fitted with steel bogies and rubber tyred wheels, for choice by the driver. There was a 16-lever signal box in the distance from 9th May 1909. It became a ground frame on 22nd November 1964 and closed on 15th February 1987. (P.D.Shannon)

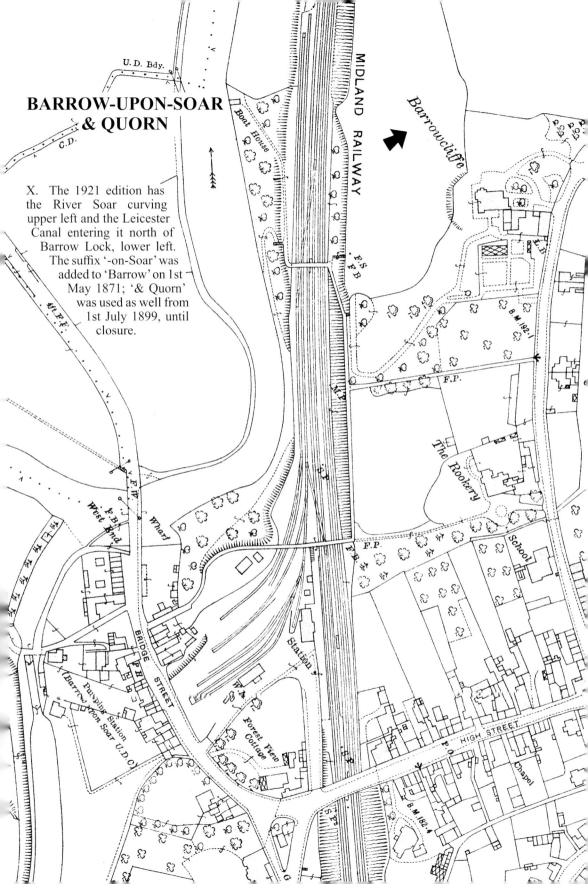

BARROW-UPON-SOAR
& QUORN

X. The 1921 edition has the River Soar curving upper left and the Leicester Canal entering it north of Barrow Lock, lower left. The suffix '-on-Soar' was added to 'Barrow' on 1st May 1871; '& Quorn' was used as well from 1st July 1899, until closure.

U. D. Bdy.

C.D.

MIDLAND RAILWAY

Barrowcliffe

Boat House

F.S.
F.B

B M 192.1

F.P.

F.F.

The Rookery

School

F.W.

West End

F.B

Wharf

F.P.
F.B

BRIDGE STREET

P.H.

Barrow upon Soar U.D.C.

Pumping Station

Forest View Cottage

Station

W.

HIGH STREET

Chapel

P.O.

B M 182.4

35.   We look north in about 1900, before two more tracks were laid behind the wall on the right. The station staff members have been supplemented by the track gang, which show shirt sleeves. The signal box in this and the next picture lasted until 9th November 1919. (J.Alsop coll.)

36.   A later southward view includes one of the new tracks, in the foreground. The steep road down to the station can be found on the left. Much local stone has been loaded on the right and is under the younger part of the footbridge. The yard had been enlarged for this traffic. (J.Alsop coll.)

37. On the right is the 1919 box, which had 24 levers and a better view. Bound for Toton Yard in May 1953 is Beyer-Garratt 2-6-6-2T no. 47986, which was built for the LMS in 1930. The goods yard here closed on 6th April 1964 and the signal box followed on 14th October 1973. (R.J.Essery coll.)

38. Bound for Nottingham in 1962 is a DMU with the original 'Cats Whiskers'. These would soon be replaced by yellow panels, to improve safety for track workers. Evident is one of Suggs Rochester pattern gas lamps, which were devoid of shadows. DMUs began on the route in the Summer of 1958. (Milepost 92½)

BARROW-UPON-SOAR

39. The building was demolished soon after closure on 4th March 1968. Southbound on 4th June 1962 is class 8F 2-8-0 no. 48356. The other two tracks pass under the right part of the bridge, which carried a public footpath, as well as passengers. The lines ran between the two walls on the right. (R.J.Essery coll.)

↑ 41. No. 158862 calls on 26th August 2017 forming the 12.26 Leicester-Lincoln train. The original station here was located beyond the tall bridge in this picture and had platforms only on the fast lines, while the new station had platforms only on the slow lines. These came into use on 27th May 1994. The 12-month figures had risen to over 98,000 by 2016. (P.D.Shannon)

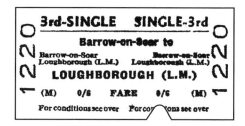

40. Grove Lane bridge is south of the station and gave pedestrians access to it. In the late evening of 1st August 2016, this collapse took place, minutes after an up train had passed along the line at about 92mph, followed by a down one at 96. A drilling machine had been used during the day to investigate reports of wet ground. Fragments of the equipment can be seen in the rubble the next day and a section of water main fell on top of it all, while both broken ends poured onto the scene. All trains were suspended, but the slow lines were soon reopened; the road was closed for 21 days. (Crown copyright/RAIB)

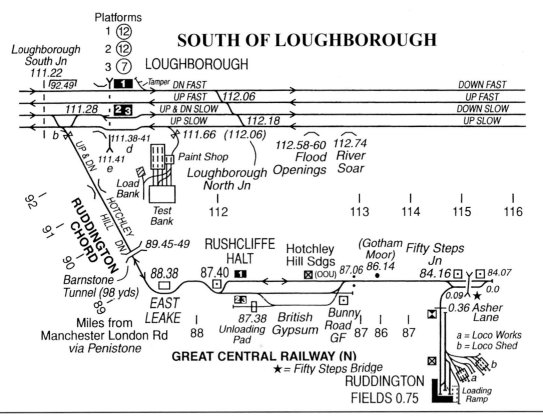

SOUTH OF LOUGHBOROUGH

Platforms

1 ⑫
2 ⑫
3 ⑦   LOUGHBOROUGH

Loughborough
South Jn
111.22

92.49	**1**	Tamper DN FAST	DOWN FAST
UP FAST	112.06	UP FAST
111.28	**2 3**	UP & DN SLOW	DOWN SLOW
UP SLOW	112.18	UP SLOW

b
d   111.38-41
111.41
e
UP & DN
RUDDINGTON CHORD
HOTCHLEY HILL DN
Load Bank
Test Bank

111.66 (112.06)
Paint Shop
Loughborough
North Jn
112

112.58-60   112.74
Flood   River
Openings   Soar

113   114   115   116

92
91
90
89

89.45-49   RUSHCLIFFE HALT
Barnstone Tunnel (98 yds)
88.38   87.40 **1**

Hotchley
Hill Sdgs
☒ (OOU)   87.06

(Gotham Moor)   Fifty Steps Jn
86.14
84.16 ⊡   Y   ⊡ 84.07

EAST LEAKE
Miles from
Manchester London Rd
via Penistone
88

2 3
87.38   British
Unloading   Gypsum
Pad

Bunny
Road
GF   87   86   87

0.09   0.0
0.09   ★
0.36 Asher Lane

a = Loco Works
b = Loco Shed

GREAT CENTRAL RAILWAY (N)
★ = Fifty Steps Bridge
RUDDINGTON FIELDS 0.75

☒
b
a
Loading Ramp

XI. The 2013 diagram has the connection on the left, near a gate. The northern section of the revived GCR carried passengers between the two stations marked HALT and FIELDS. The River Soar supplied water troughs from 1907 until the 1960s. The gypsum traffic began in 1898. The second signal box is shown as Out of Use. Its 18-lever frame was used from the 1940s to 4th January 1970. Passenger service ceased on the route in 1969 and this short part reopened in 2013. The halt, however, had closed on 4th March 1963. (©TRACKmaps)

42. Lower right is one of the two platforms on our route; the other two tracks can be seen through the fence. We look southeast in 1949 as class B1 4-6-2 no. 1248 *Geoffrey Gibbs* runs on the former GCR line. The site is top right on map XII. The bridge was dismantled in 1980; the curve can be seen in picture 13 in the *Loughborough to Nottingham* album. The route to Ruddington is on map XI above. (M.J.Stretton coll.)

43. A replacement bridge was craned into place on 3rd September 2017 to enable the GCR to be re-connected to its northern part. The revival of the southern section to Leicester began between Loughborough and Quorn & Woodhouse, with trains operating from 23rd March 1974. Rothley saw its first train on 8th September 1975. The Belgrave & Birstall route took passengers from 15th November 1990, but the station had been demolished in 1977, due to vandalism. A new station at Leicester North was opened on 3rd July 1991. (Great Central Railway)

LOUGHBOROUGH

XII. The 1938 edition at 6ins to 1 mile has the ex-MR line and its station upper right. The former GCR route is top to bottom. To enable this to be closed, but maintain a freight link with Ruddington, a curve was opened between the two on 8th April 1974, from east to north.

Falcon Works was used by the Brush Group, Hawker Siddeley, Brush Traction and Petters Oil Engines for many years. The Skoda Group took control in 2001 and Melrose in 2008. There were about 5000 workers here by 1973. Loughborough Gas Works started in 1836 and used 7882 tons of coal in 1900, rising to about 40,000 tons per annum in 1950, all without a railway connection.

44. A late Victorian panorama has much of the footbridge hidden by steam, but includes a fine choice of horse-drawn transport. On the left is the goods yard and its crane, which was rated at 10-ton capacity. (R.J.Essery coll.)

45. A Peerless steam railmotor is seen on trial on 2nd June 1905. Four were used between Dublin and Howth. The bridge conceals the words BRUSH ELECTRICAL. 'Light Company' had been added in 1889, but this was replaced by 'Engineering' later. Products included railway and tramway locomotives, plus stock. Battery powered milk delivery floats, bus bodies, aircraft wings and body parts formed the main output, until 1957. (J.Alsop coll.)

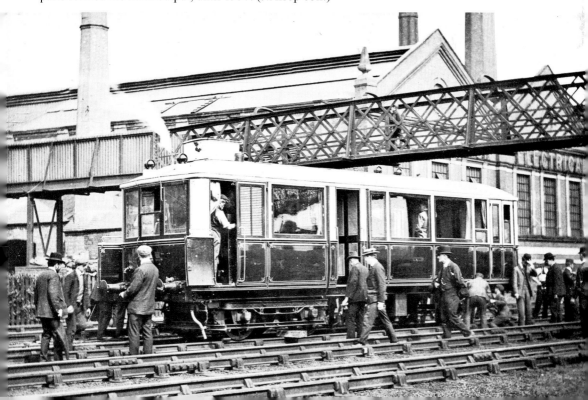

46.   The station name was Loughborough from 5th May 1840 to 1922, then Loughborough Town until 8th July 1923 and Loughborough Midland to 3rd May 1970. This view from the 1950s includes a Royal Mail van having just unloaded a trolley load of bags. The coachworks here closed in 1952. In 1957, Brush Electrical Machines were bought up by Hawker Siddeley to become the Brush Electrical Engineering Company Limited. (Milepost 92½)

← 47. Public goods traffic ceased on 1st May 1972, but three sidings in the left background plus a loading loop were long used by Amey Roadstone. One in the centre distance was still a private siding for Herbert Morris Ltd, when this photo was taken on 6th July 1975. The firm produced conveyor belts, massive cranes and much else. By then, there were over 2000 employees. The view features no. 45144 with the 09.50 from Nottingham to St. Pancras and the Falcon Works, which was used by various Brush engineering companies from 1889. The falcon (top right) later flew to the National Tramway Museum for retirement. (T.Heavyside)

48. We move further north on the same day to see more of the engineering facilities. There were some sidings between the buildings, running north from wagon turntables, for many years. Brush Bagnall Traction was involved in producing class 30, 31, 47, 56, 57, 60, 89 and 92 locomotives for BR. No. 44004 is working an engineers train of scrap. (T.Heavyside)

Midland Railway
Loughboro' to
BARROW
SECOND CLASS
This Ticket is issued subject to the regulations & Conditions stated in the Company's Time Tables & Bills
Barrow   Barrow

49. The first station was southeast of the bridge until 13th May 1872. Close to it was the goods yard; it lasted there until 31st March 1879, although its successor had opened in 1875. The signal box had 44 levers and is near the end of the train. It was in use from 19th June 1892 until 11th April 1987. A class 45 is heading an express from St Pancras on 5th September 1981. (J.Whitehouse)

50. Modernisation took place in 2010-12, but the early buildings and canopies were retained. Platform 3, the former down slow, now deals with both up and down local passenger trains. Since 1993, the up slow line no longer had a platform, saving the cost of a footbridge over these lines. Here, DMU no. 158785 departs with the 13.26 Leicester-Lincoln, whilst Meridian no. 222009 arrives at platform 1 with the 12.26 St Pancras to Sheffield. It is 31st March 2016, when the 12-monthly passenger figure was around 1.3m. (A.C.Hartless)

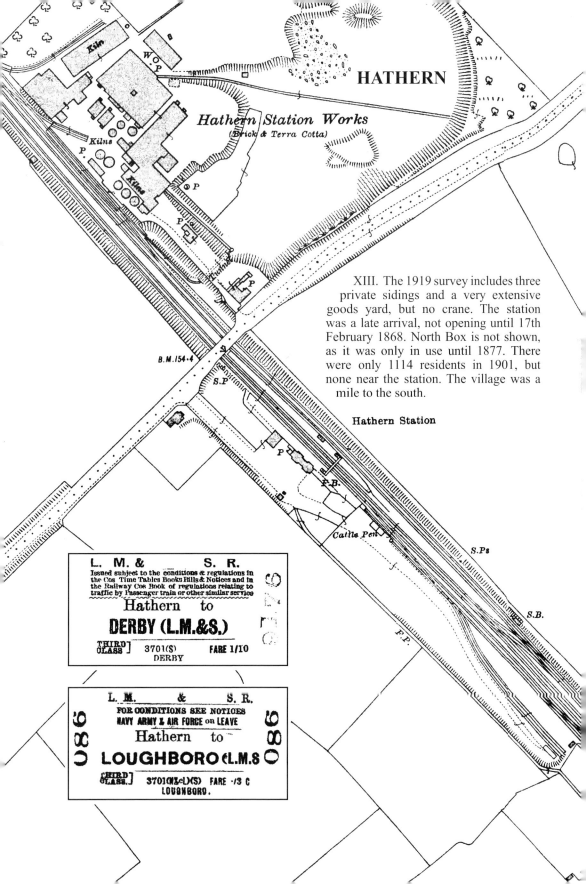

HATHERN

Hathern Station Works
(Brick & Terra Cotta)

XIII. The 1919 survey includes three private sidings and a very extensive goods yard, but no crane. The station was a late arrival, not opening until 17th February 1868. North Box is not shown, as it was only in use until 1877. There were only 1114 residents in 1901, but none near the station. The village was a mile to the south.

Hathern Station

B.M.154·4

S.P.

Cattle Pen

S.Ps

S.B.

F.P.

L. M. & S. R.
Issued subject to the conditions & regulations in the Cos Time Tables Books Bills & Notices and in the Railway Cos Book of regulations relating to traffic by Passenger train or other similar service
Hathern   to
DERBY (L.M.&S.)
THIRD CLASS]   3701(S)   FARE 1/10
DERBY

L. M.   &   S. R.
FOR CONDITIONS SEE NOTICES
NAVY ARMY & AIR FORCE on LEAVE
Hathern   to
LOUGHBORO (L.M.S
THIRD CLASS]   3701(NEcL)(S)   FARE -/3 C
LOUGHBORO.

51.   This view north is from the road bridge prior to about 1919. An MR 4-4-0 'Compound' runs through with an express bound for London. The private siding shown on the map is not present, but its point is. The hut contained a ground frame, which was in use until 1928. (R.J.Essery coll.)

52.   The 2.24pm Leicester to Manchester is approaching on 25th May 1949, headed by class 5 4-6-0 no. 44846. It is near the 1892 South Box, which lost its suffix in 1958. It had 32 levers and was worked until 28th September 1969. The main building was in use for Bed & Breakfast from April 2012; tel. 01509 646463. (R.J.Essery coll.)

L. M. & S. R.   Ticket for
PERAMBULATOR &c.
in charge of Passenger
Hathern   to
LOUGHBORO

NAME OF ARTICLE
PRAM

Carriage Paid!' s. 5d.

F 144

↓ 53. The goods yard and the station shed closed on 4th January 1960. Passing with empty mineral wagons on 9th June 1962 is class 8F 2-8-0 no. 48625. There were water troughs south of here for filling tenders at speed. They had an average length of 575 yards and were in place here from about 1904 to 1966. (Milepost 92½)

KEGWORTH

XIV. The 1921 issue includes another spacious goods yard, plus a connection at the top to Lord Belper's Branch, which opened in about 1890 and closed on 8th January 1972, having served the two-mile long New Kingston Gypsum Mine line. This passed under the main line and ran east, to the quarry. Most of the work was undertaken by *Lady Angela*, a Peckett 0-4-0ST born in 1926. All wagons had to travel via the goods yard; there was no direct connection to a main line. Traffic ceased on 17th April 1971. Kegworth Gas & Coke Co. took 525 tons in 1900, had no railway siding and later (pre-1938) took a supply of gas from Long Eaton instead of making its own; an early example of a pipeline taking traffic away from the railway.

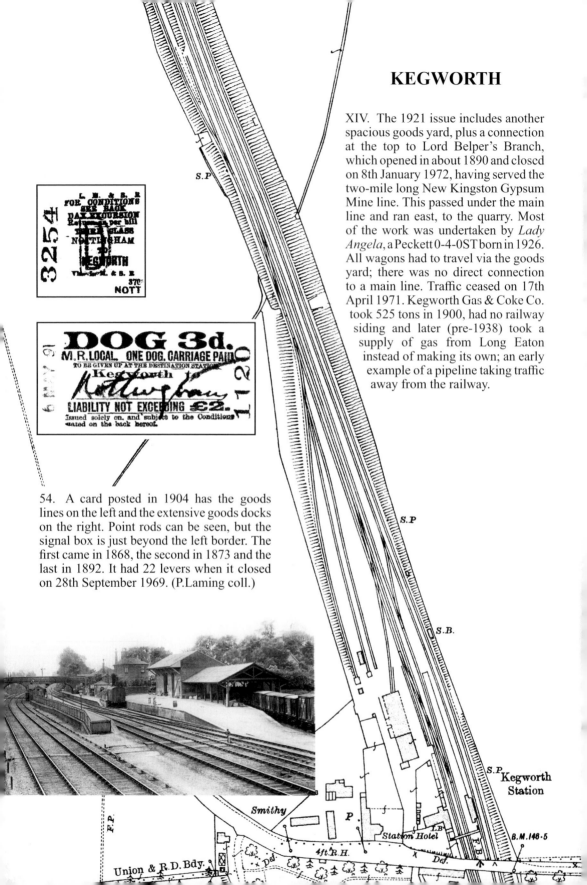

54. A card posted in 1904 has the goods lines on the left and the extensive goods docks on the right. Point rods can be seen, but the signal box is just beyond the left border. The first came in 1868, the second in 1873 and the last in 1892. It had 22 levers when it closed on 28th September 1969. (P.Laming coll.)

55. Class 5 4-6-0 no. 44663 hurries south, some time in the late 1950s. At least the cab and the smokebox are clean. Flat bottom rails and well-tended gardens were recent developments. (M.J.Stretton coll.)

56. A southward panorama from 1st October 1967 features the station buildings and the end-loading dock, used by the horse-drawn coaches of the wealthy and the agricultural equipment of others. All goods traffic ceased here on 5th July 1965, hence the weeds. Passenger service ended on 4th March 1968. (R.J.Essery coll.)

← 57. No. 58004 departs from Ratcliffe Power Station with 43 empty Merry-Go-Round hoppers for Toton yard on 24th April 1984. The power station was commissioned in 1968 and received its coal Merry-Go-Round style right from the start. It also forwarded fly ash by rail to Fletton, near Peterborough. No. 58004 was less than a year old when this photograph was taken; it was withdrawn in 2002. (P.D.Shannon)

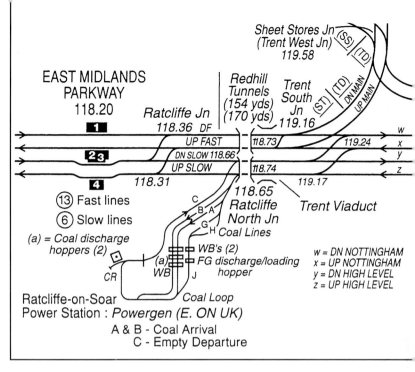

XV. The 2013 diagram shows the five weighbridges as WB and the cripple siding as CR. The other initials are explained thereon, except the circles. These show the number of standard coaches acceptable in the platforms. The connections came into use on 8th October 1967. There had been a signal box nearby from 1893 to 28th September 1969. (©TRACKmaps)

58. Most of the eight gigantic cooling towers were recorded on 25th April 2002, along with no. 66175, hauling a gypsum train bound for Hotchley Hill. The works has a 653ft tall chimney and four coal-fired boilers made by Babcock & Wilcox, each of which drives a 500 megawatt Parsons generator set. This gives the station a total generating capacity of 2116MW, which is enough electricity to meet the needs of approximately 2.02m homes. (M.Turvey)

EAST MIDLANDS PARKWAY

59.   Pictured on 9th July 2009 is Meridian no. 222018 with the 13.47 Sheffield-St Pancras. The heavily engineered qualities of the station are immediately apparent. It had opened on 26th January of that year. Thereafter, around 0.3m passengers used the station annually. About 24,000 were changing trains. (A.C.Hartless)

60. The station has a car park for 850 vehicles. On 11th February 2009, Unit 1 became the first UK 500 MW coal-fired unit to run for 250,000 hours. On 2nd April 2009, E.ON UK announced that it had installed a 68-panel solar photovoltaic array at the power station to help heat and light the admin block, saving an estimated 6.3 tonnes of carbon dioxide per year. It is 5th April 2017 and no. 66704 growls past with a train from Toton North Yard to Whitemoor Yard. (J.Whitehouse)

SOUTH OF TRENT

Red Hill Tunnel

61.   This well-known engraving is from 1886 and shows the north end of the tunnel and the busy River Trent. The castellated portal buildings were used for staff accommodation. This style was demanded by the owner of Thrumpton Hall and the adjacent land. (F.S.Williams)

62.   The second tunnel was opened in 1893, to the east of the original one. Here is the new steel lattice bridge. The cattle take no interest in the three fine clerestory coaches, probably in about 1900. (J.Alsop coll.)

63.   The north end is seen again, this time on 19th April 1997. Ex-LNER class A2 4-6-2 no. 60532 *Blue Peter* works a special north: 'The Severn & Stour', a Hertfordshire Rail Tour. (R.J.Stewart-Smith)

64.   A panorama from 2nd March 2005 is limited by vegetation neglect and no boats are evident. A class 43 is reducing its speed, as it approaches the complex junctions. The towers double their purpose with a few transmitters. (J.Whitehouse)

TRENT

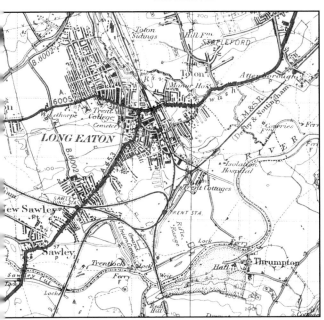

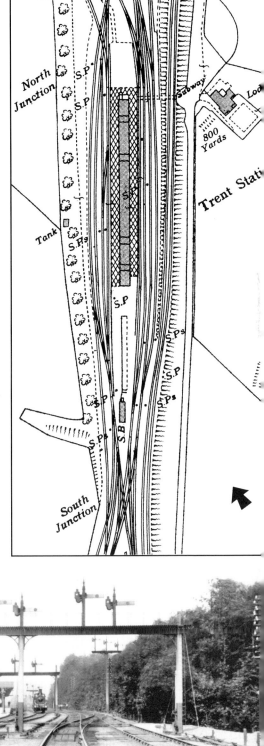

XVI. The 1946 edition is shown at 1in to 1 mile and has our route from the lower to the right border. On the left is the 1839 line from Derby and at the top is the 1847 route to Ilkeston and beyond. All were ex-MR. The River Trent meanders across the extract and is partially canalised. Long Eaton Junction station was southeast of the town until 1862.

➜ XVII. The 1938 survey has the high level goods lines on an embankment, to the right of the station. Access to it was via the subway.

65. Trent Station South Box opened on 3rd March 1901 and lasted until 28th September 1969, when it had 69 levers. Station North Box is also shown on the map; it had 75 levers and closed on the same day.
(R.J.Essery coll.)

66. Looking north in about 1910, we have three pairs of tracks before reaching the platform. The pair on the right were added in 1901 and used until 1968. They enabled northern trains to bypass the station. (J.Alsop coll.)

67. Class 4P 4-4-0 no. 40931 departs with a stopping train from Nottingham to Derby, some time in the 1950s. The station was open from 1st May 1862 until 1st January 1968 and was mainly used by people changing trains at this important 'cross roads'. (R.Humm coll.)

68.   We are north of the station with a mineral train running in on the bypass line. The parallel high level line can be glimpsed in front of the loco; it runs on the other side of the row of cottages in this view from the 1950s. (R.J.Essery coll.)

69.   Bound for Derby on 3rd May 1958, this 3-car Cravens DMU is starting on the long curve to Sawley Junction. During the heavy demands of WWII, Permissive Working was allowed on some lines. This meant that drivers could proceed slowly and look out for the tail of the train in front. (R.Humm coll.)

70. The up 'Thames-Clyde Express' is awaiting departure, some time in 1959. The name came into use in 1927. No. 45590 is a 'Jubilee' class 4-6-0, named *Travancore*. Few such busy junctions could manage with just one island platform; it certainly pleased passengers, as did the floral displays. (R.S.Carpenter coll.)

Other views can be seen in *Nuneaton to Loughborough*, **in pictures 99 to 102.**

71. We finish by looking north at North Junction, with Station North Box prominent and North Curve on the left. The Commission's House is on the right. The Commission was an MR term denoting who was in charge. Two crossovers are evident, as well. (J.Langford coll.)

72. This is where the Nottingham line diverges from the route north along the Erewash Valley. The pronunciation is usually 'Error-wash'. The Erewash Canal is part of a crossroads in the waterway system near here. The 1893 box had 36 levers and became Meadow Lane Crossing shunting frame on 28th September 1969, closing on 16th July 1978, when Trent Power Signal Box came into use. (R.Humm coll.)

Attenborough Junction

73. This and the last picture are from 22nd March 1969. The 1900 box had a 30-lever frame and functioned to 28th September 1969, also. Staff transport was still two-wheeled and fire buckets have been reduced from three to one. (R.Humm coll.)

ATTENBOROUGH

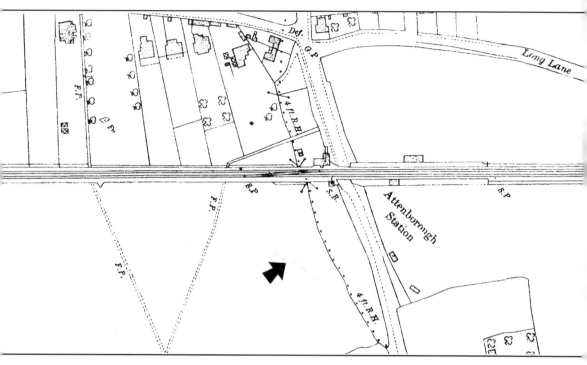

XVIII. A halt called Attenborough Gate was open west of the level crossing from 1856 to 1st November 1858. The station came into use on 1st September 1864. It was renamed Chilwell briefly in 1937, but residents objected. They numbered only 1176 in 1901.

74. The platforms had been greatly lengthened during World War I to cope with trains for vast numbers of workers at a military depot called Chilwell, established west of the station. Access was from the level crossing, to the left of the camera. Originally Ministry of Munitions, National Filling Factory No. 6, construction of the depot commenced on 13th September 1915. Production began in March 1916. The depot and rail system closed on 31st March 1982. (P.Laming coll.)

75.   In the 1970s, there was usually one train each way per hour, weekdays only. The 1894 signal box had 22 levers in use until 7th December 1969. It just controlled the level crossing from then until 27th June 1982. (R.Humm coll.)

76.   No. 170103 in Central Trains livery calls at Attenborough with the 13.00 Nottingham to Cardiff Central train on 17th December 2005. The platforms had once been much longer. They took seven cars, as seen. The WD Depot had been busy during WWII and during the Suez Crisis. It had extensive sidings and several locomotives. The workmen's service to it ceased on 4th November 1963. In 1938, it was listed as the Royal Army Ordnance Vehicle Reserve Depot. (P.D.Shannon)

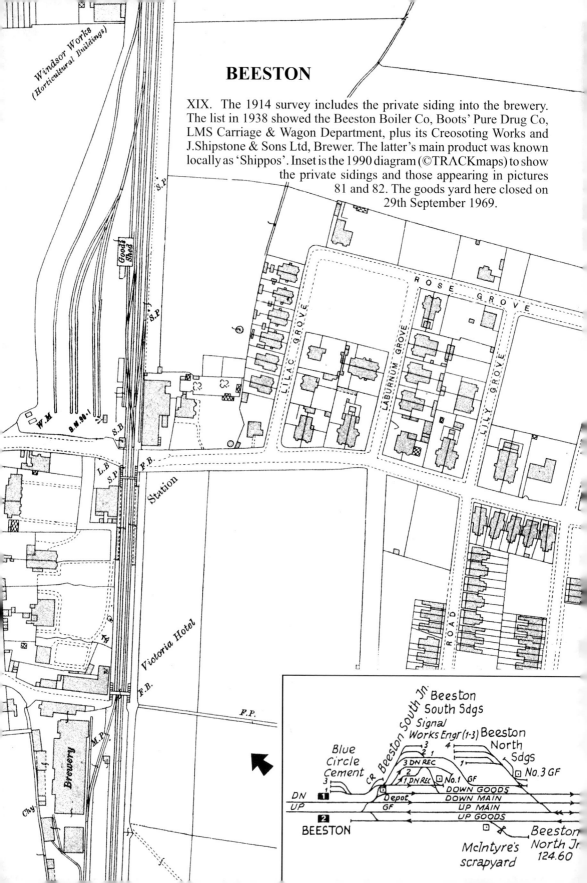

BEESTON

XIX. The 1914 survey includes the private siding into the brewery. The list in 1938 showed the Beeston Boiler Co, Boots' Pure Drug Co, LMS Carriage & Wagon Department, plus its Creosoting Works and J.Shipstone & Sons Ltd, Brewer. The latter's main product was known locally as 'Shippos'. Inset is the 1990 diagram (©TRACKmaps) to show the private sidings and those appearing in pictures 81 and 82. The goods yard here closed on 29th September 1969.

Windsor Works
(Horticultural Buildings)

Goods Shed

S.P.

S.P.

S.P.

W.M.

B.M.90·1

S.B

L.B

S.P.

F.B.

Station

Victoria Hotel

F.B.

F.P.

Brewery

Chy.

M.P.

LILAC GROVE

LABURNUM GROVE

ROSE GROVE

LILY GROVE

ROAD

Beeston South Jn.
Beeston South Sdgs
Signal Works Engr (1-3)
Beeston North Sdgs
CR
Blue Circle Cement
Depot
GF
No.1 GF
No.3 GF
DN
UP
BEESTON
DOWN GOODS
DOWN MAIN
UP MAIN
UP GOODS
McIntyre's scrapyard
Beeston North Jr.
124.60
DN REC

77. A local train for Nottingham is arriving in about 1910, a time when all heads should be covered. The locality was developing as a suburb and road transport was still for the wealthy few. The main building dates from 1847 and it received Listing in 1987. (J.Alsop coll.)

78. A very long mineral train is behind class 9F 2-10-0 no. 92128, some time in 1958. It is passing the goods yard, which closed on 29th September 1969. The box had 25 levers and a gate wheel. Built in 1891, it lasted until 7th December 1969. A bridge replaced the level crossing in 1969. (Colour-Rail.com)

79.   It is 16th August 1967 and a young lady gazes at the wicket gate as they were safer to use than walking in the road. They were always released before the main gates. The complex footbridge was often the quickest way. In 1973, the Harwich-Manchester boat trains were re-routed to call here. The bridge was busy quite often, as the gates were moved about 100 times a day, in the steam era. (R.J.Essery/R.S.Carpenter)

80.   A visit on 17th December 2005 finds Central Trains unit no. 158862 calling with the 09.45 Cardiff Central-Nottingham, while a Midland Mainline 'Meridian' unit forms the 12.52 Nottingham-St Pancras. Both platforms could take seven cars. The population had expanded from 8960 in 1901 to 57,700 in 1961. Passengers per annum numbered around 0.5m in 2011-16. In 2017, there were two through trains to St Pancras and one to Bournemouth amongst the many shorter journeys each weekday. (P.D.Shannon)

EAST OF BEESTON

81.   Beeston South Junction Box is seen in the early 1930s. It had 60 levers and functioned from 21st September 1930 until 7th December 1969. Beeston Sidings had eight numbered signal boxes. (R.S.Carpenter)

82.   Nos 20168 and 20193 haul eastbound empties past Beeston Yard on 16th September 1982. Stored beyond the coal wagons are class 317s for the St Pancras to Bedford route, once known as the Bedpan Line. (T.Heavyside)

83. No. 40194 passes Beeston Freightliner terminal, with track sections bound for Rugby on 3rd August 1984. The terminal operated from 29th June 1969 until 6th April 1987, but handled just one daily feeder service to and from Birmingham in its later years. The sidings between the Freightliner terminal and the main line were the gathering point for wagonload freight in the Nottingham area; on this occasion they hold ballast hoppers and ferry vans. (P.D.Shannon)

L. M. & S. R.
Issued subject to the conditions & regulations in the Coa Time Tables Books Bills & Notices and in the Railway Coa Book of regulations relating to traffic by Passenger train or other similar service

Beeston to
ATTENBORO

THIRD] 3608 (S   FARE -/7½
CLASS   ATTENBORO

4759

L. M. & S. R. For conditions see notice.
MONTHLY RET
Valid as advertised
THIRD CLASS
Leicester
TO
ATTENBORO
fare 4/10C   3407 (MR)
LEICESTER

L. M. & S. R.
MONTHLYRET
THIRD CLASS
Attenboro
TO
LEICESTER(LMS)
Fare 4/10C

2703   2703

84. No. 66145 pulls out of the up loop with the 11.33 Humber Refinery-Kingsbury oil train on 20th April 2011. The former Freightliner terminal was in use as a railway infrastructure depot, assembling points and crossings for Network Rail. The small yard between the depot and the main line had been reduced to a simple run-round loop. (P.D.Shannon)

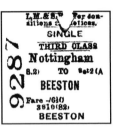

85. The engine sheds are on the diagram; all three were round houses, with access from the far end. The code was 16A in 1948-63 and 16D until closure to steam in 1965. They housed 144 locos in 1950 and 96 in 1959. The photo is from 30th January 1966. Final closure was in November 1967. (R.Humm coll.)

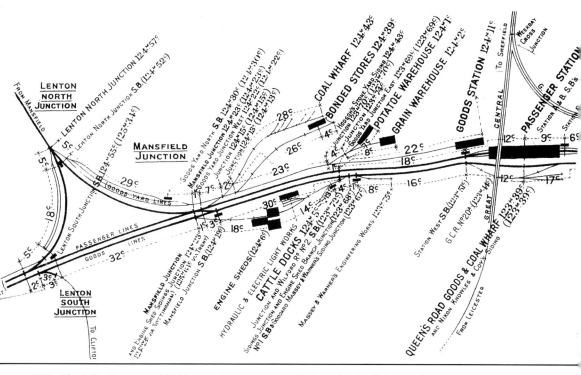

XX. The MR diagram of 1912 reveals the complex links to its facilities on the approach to its main station.

86. Mansfield Junction box had a 65-lever frame and is seen on 29th March 1969. The 1902 structure had been enlarged in 1933 and closed on 7th December 1969. Lenton South Junction Box was at the east end of the triangular junction and its 53-lever frame was not used after 17th May 1981. Wilford Road Box was the nearest to Nottingham station and its 50-lever frame was worked from 1935 to 1969. It is close to the left border of the next map. (R.Humm coll.)

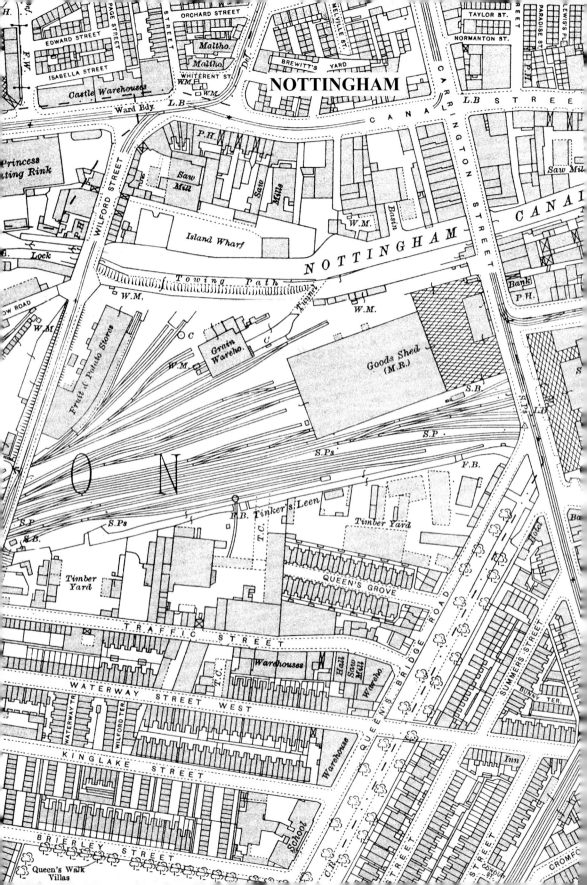

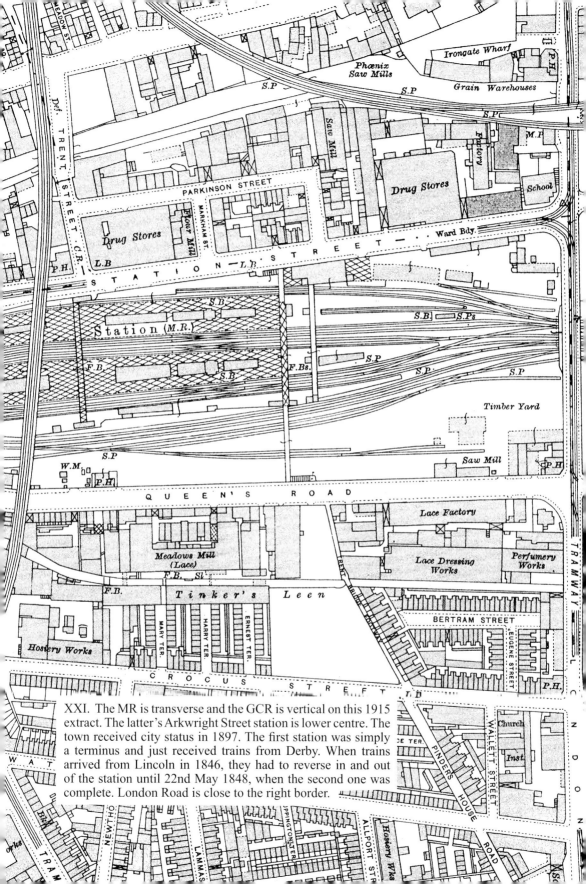

Phœnix
Saw Mills

Irongate Wharf

Grain Warehouses

P.H

S.P

S.P

S.P

M.P

Factory

Drug Stores

School

PARKINSON STREET

Saw Mill

Def.

TRENT STREET CR.

Flour Mill

MARKHAM ST.

Drug Stores

Ward Bdy.

P.H

L.B

STATION — L.B — STREET — L.B —

S.B

Station (M.R.)

S.B

S.Ps

F.B.

S.B

F.Bs.

S.P

S.P

S.P

Timber Yard

S.P

Saw Mill

P.H

W.M.

P.H

S.P

QUEEN'S ROAD

Lace Factory

Meadows Mill
(Lace)

Lace Dressing
Works

Perfumery
Works

F.B. Sl.

F.B.

Tinker's Leen

BERTRAM STREET

EUGENE STREET

P.H

Hosiery Works

MARY TER.

HARRY TER.

ERNEST TER.

TRENT ROAD

TRAMWAY LONDON

CROCUS STREET

WATT

NEWTHO

LAMMAS

IPPINGTON STER.

ALLPORT STR.

Hosiery Wks.

ROAD

Church

Inst.

CE TER.

PINDERS HOUSE

WALLETT STREET

XXI. The MR is transverse and the GCR is vertical on this 1915 extract. The latter's Arkwright Street station is lower centre. The town received city status in 1897. The first station was simply a terminus and just received trains from Derby. When trains arrived from Lincoln in 1846, they had to reverse in and out of the station until 22nd May 1848, when the second one was complete. London Road is close to the right border.

87.   Here is the frontage of the third station, soon after it was officially opened on 17th January 1904. The style was termed Edwardian Baroque Revival. There is evidence of the tramway, which was in use from 1901 to 1936. Glass doors were fitted in 2014. The suffix MIDLAND was applied to the station name from 18th June 1951 to 6th May 1970. It had been CITY for six months earlier. (J.Alsop coll.)

88.   The port-cochère area is seen on the morning of the royal visit on 24th June 1914. On the right is the base of the clock tower, seen in the previous picture. The city had many great architectural joys, notably its castle set on a rocky red sandstone eminence nearby. The original station's gate posts could still be seen in 2016, close to the pedestrian's entrance to the Magistrate's Courts. (J.Alsop coll.)

89. The memorable clock tower appears again in this panorama of the commercial traffic hub. Witness some of the local traffic, but the items changing trains usually did so under a roof. BR employed 85 horses here as late as 1950. (R.Humm coll.)

→ 90. It is 27th April 1957 and no. 62535 simmers, with a leaking injector. It is a class D16 4-4-0 of the Eastern Region. The former GCR is above the second coach; the van was for parcel and/or mail traffic. The lattice structure was dismantled in 1980.
(M.J.Stretton coll.)

2nd-SINGLE	SINGLE-2nd
Nottingham (Midland) to	
Nottingham (Midland) Netherfield & Colwick	Nottingham (Midland) Netherfield & Colwick
NETHERFIELD & COLWICK	
(M) 0/9 Fare (M)	
For conditions see over For conditions see over	

6654   6654

L. M.   &   S. R.
FOR CONDITIONS SEE NOTICES NAVY ARMY & AIR FORCE on LEAVE
NOTTINGHAM TO
MARKET HARBORO'
[THIRD CLASS] 3610(N&eLS) FARE 3/5 L MARKET HAR.

3996   3996

↓ 91. Another 1957 view and this includes the two footbridges shown on the map. Each has its own lift shaft and the further one is for public use. At each end are steps to the nearest streets. Trolleybuses ran to the station in 1927-66. (Stations UK)

↘ 92. This view west is from 7th June 1969 and features the side of the lower building seen in picture 89. Station West Box, shown, had 53 levers. Station A had 12 and 22, Station B, 12 and 36, Station East, 72, and London Road Junction, 86. They all lasted until Trent Power Signal Box took over in 1969. (R.Humm coll.)

93.   View no. 89 is repeated, but on 16th September 1982. Just five tracks remain, but the station facade and clock tower were kept. Running west is a class 08 diesel shunter, with a barrier wagon for safety reasons. A severe fire early on 12th January 2018 ruined the extensively refurbished booking hall and closed the station for the day. (T.Heavyside)

94.   On 30th June 2006, unit no. 156414 calls with the 16.40 Lincoln-Leicester service, while no. 170109 waits to depart with the 17.26 to Worksop. Servicing facilities occupy the space vacated by the former middle track. London Road Bridge is in the background and the junction is just beyond it. A major rebuild took place which involved six miles of new track, 143 new signals and a new bay platform, set into no. 4. The full service was restored on 27th August 2013. (P.D.Shannon)

95.   No. 43073 is working to St Pancras International on 13th March 2009. A new bridge came into use for the southern extension of the Nottingham Express Transit on 25th August 2015. Trams were able to stop on it and escalators plus a lift were available. Until then, trams had terminated in Station Road. Annual railway figures were over 7m by 2016. (J.Whitehouse)

For other views of the area see *Nottingham to Boston, Nottingham to Lincoln, Loughborough to Nottingham, Kettering to Nottingham, Nottinghamshire & Derby Tramways* **and** *Nottingham Trolleybuses.*

2. Syston Junction to Melton Mowbray

Syston East Junction

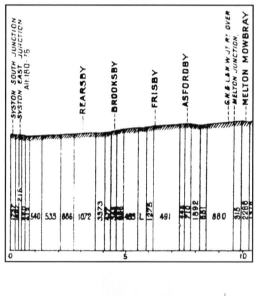

96.   It is 5th August 1961 and class B1 4-6-0 no. 61283 is accelerating over the junction with a Leicester to Peterborough train. Waiting on the 1854 small radius curve is class 9F 2-10-0 no. 92056, with freight from Toton Yard to Wellingborough. (M.J.Stretton coll.)

97.   Syston East Junction Box of November 1927 is seen on 6th August 1968. It had a 25-lever frame and closed on 2nd September 1973. Here we are looking towards the main line. The curve to the left opened in 1846 for Melton Mowbray trains. (R.Humm coll.)

QUENIBOROUGH

98. This is an interesting location, but it was never a public station. The site became a Royal Ordnance Filling Factory in 1942 and a two-platform private station was built on a loop off the main line, presumably for workers' trains from Leicester and Melton. The factory closed in 1959, and the site is now the new village of East Goscote. This and the next picture were taken on 6th August 1968. (R.Humm coll.)

99. The box had a 65-lever frame and opened with the station on 9th November 1941. It remained in use until 19th December 1976. Its concrete roof was designed to resist enemy bombs. Construction work was undertaken by Holloway Brothers of London, starting on 8th November 1940 and completed by July 1941. The depot had three standard gauge Bagnall 0-4-0STs and a Fowler 0-4-0 diesel delivered new to work the rail system. All these were sold or transferred elsewhere by 1952, when replaced by two virtually new Andrew Barclay 0-4-0 diesels, transferred from Longmoor in 1946. These two worked the rail traffic until the factory closed in 1959, when they were transferred to Bicester for further use. (R.Humm coll.)

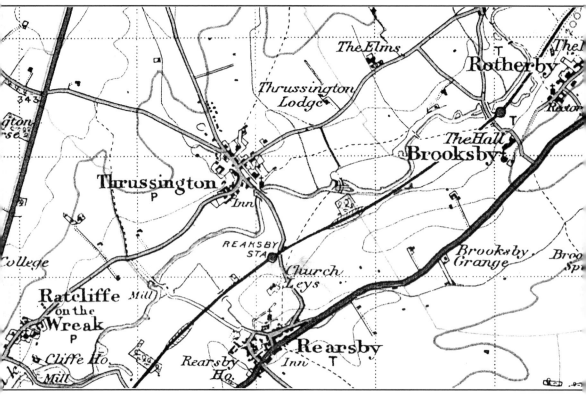

XXII. The 1946 map shows the position of this and the next station to the villages nearby. Both had opened on 1st September 1846. Two mills were nearby.

100. A well-dressed group wait by the wicket gate to cross before the main gates are opened. Some notable chimneys and barge boards can be examined and enjoyed in this southward view. (LOSA)

101. This undated record provides fine details of the splendid stone work. Much of the accommodation was for the station master and his family, often large in Victorian times. The unroofed section on the right was provided for the use of gentlemen. Trains stopped here until 2nd April 1951. (R.Humm coll.)

XXIII. The 1883 survey reveals little habitation nearby. There were 427 residents recorded in the census of 1901 and 677 in 1961.

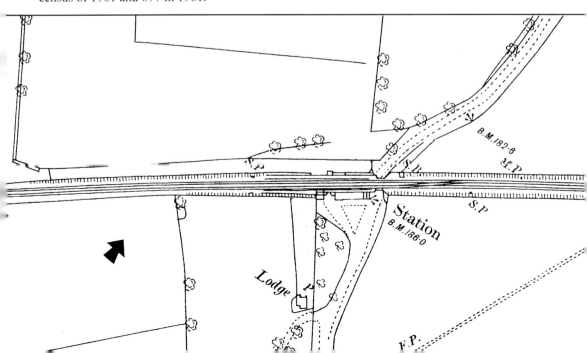

102. Seen on 14th August 1962, this 12-lever signal box was open from 1899 to 22nd January 1967. It was the second one to be provided here; the map shows the first. Run annually for several years, this coastal special was hauled by no. 45264, a class 5 4-6-0. They mostly ran to Skegness. (M.J.Stretton coll.)

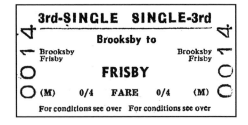

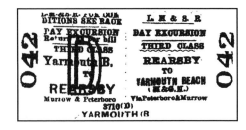

BROOKSBY

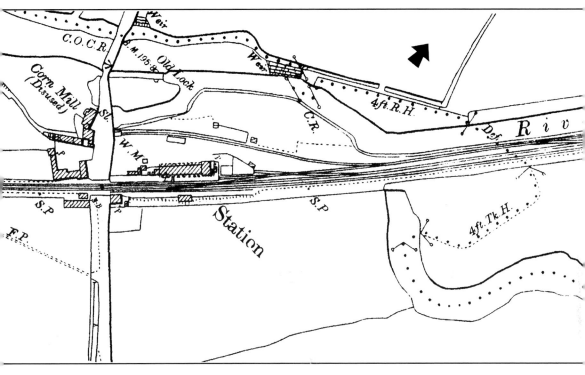

XXIV. The 1903 survey includes evidence of a weighing machine, which was for use by road vehicles. The dots of the parish boundary show the water course before its realignment for improvement of supply to the mill and to allow passage of commercial boats.

103. An early postcard includes the standard trailing points for safe access to the goods yard; also to be seen is part of the goods loop. The raised end of the platform served the end loading dock. Residents numbered 73 in 1901. (J.Alsop coll.)

104. This was the second signal box and it was in use from 4th January 1896 until 22nd January 1967. All windows were fitted with small pieces of glazing, for security and economy. Float glass was expensive and liable to damage. (P.Laming coll.)

105. The lanterns were home to paraffin lamps after dark. The fenestrated chimneys were status symbols, but could be enjoyed by few. The 7.40am from Peterborough to Leicester is seen on 19th June 1961, two weeks before station closure. Power is provided by no. 76030, a class 4 2-6-0 of BR origin. The goods yard was in use until 4th May 1964. (M.J.Stretton coll.)

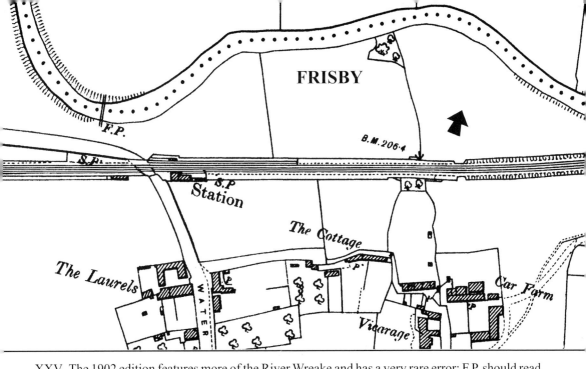

XXV. The 1902 edition features more of the River Wreake and has a very rare error; F.P. should read F.B. Many issues showed 'Frisby on the Wreake' as the village name. The 1901 census recorded 341 residing there.

106. The 12.10pm Peterborough to Leicester was photographed on 27th June 1959. Repairs are in progress, but trains ceased to call after 3rd July 1961. It had opened four months after the line, on 1st January 1847. Until then, trains only called on market days. (Colour-Rail.com)

107. The box had 10 levers and a gate wheel. It came into use on 23rd February 1941 and is seen on 22nd April 1961, as class 8F 2-8-0 no. 48319 from Toton Shed runs through with a down mineral train. (R.Humm coll.)

108. A three-car class 120 cross-country DMU recedes towards Melton Mowbray at the site of Frisby station on 14th April 1984. Frisby box was retained to oversee the minor road level crossing; it became a fringe box when the Leicester area was resignalled in 1987 and it then received a panel. (P.D.Shannon)

ASFORDBY

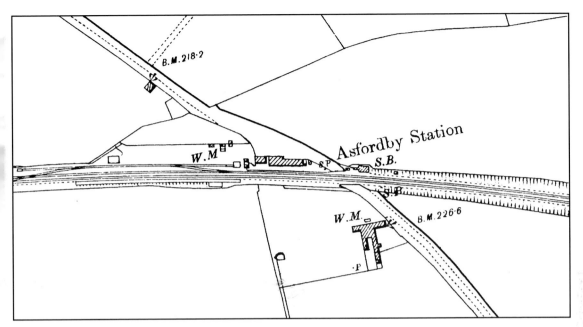

XXVI. The 1902 survey shows the station to be remote from habitation. It housed 1062 in 1901, but grew to accommodate 7582 by 1961. It opened with the line as Kirby, became As**h**fordby in 1857 and Asfordby in 1861. It had the suffix 'late Kirby' in some publications.

109. The station is seen some time after its closure on 2nd April 1951; the advertisements and lights had long gone. The small goods yard remained in use until 4th May 1964. North of the village was Asfordby Colliery. It came into full production in April 1995, after 11 years of preparation, but closed in August 1997, a few days after a 120 metre rockface was crushed under a fall and flood, destroying £6m worth of equipment. Coal trains can be seen in pictures 81 and 82 of our *Kettering to Nottingham* album. (R.Humm coll.)

110. Peak class diesel no. D114 is passing Asfordby signal box with the 1.20pm Peterborough to Leicester on 17th June 1962. This is the second signal box; it opened on 21st January 1899 and its 16-lever frame was in use until 18th December 1966. The photographer is posing as a lamp man, on the other signal. (M.J.Stretton coll.)

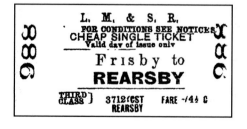

L. M. & S. R.
FOR CONDITIONS SEE NOTICES
CHEAP SINGLE TICKET
Valid day of issue only
Frisby to
REARSBY
THIRD CLASS   3712 CST   FARE -/4½ C
REARSBY

2nd-SINGLE   SINGLE-2nd
Frisby to
Frisby
Melton Mowbray   Melton Mowbray
(Town)   (Town)
MELTON MOWBRAY
(TOWN)
0/5   Fare   0/5   (M)
For conditions see over   For conditions see over

EAST OF ASFORDBY

Melton Junction

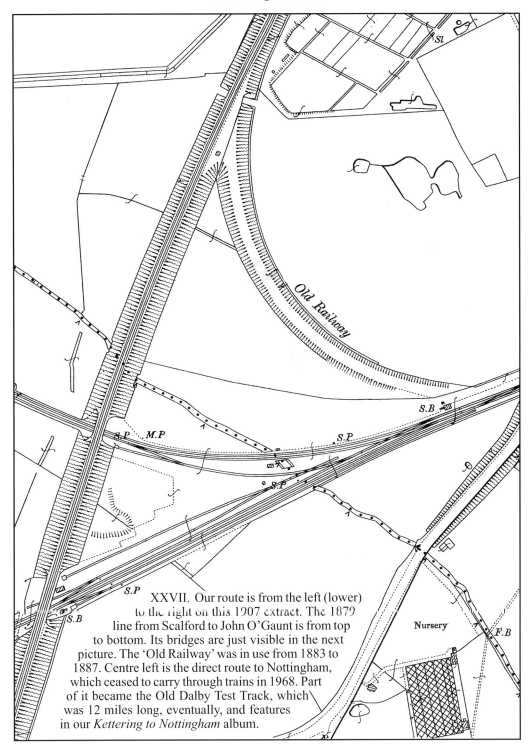

Old Railway

S.B

S.P   M.P   S.P

S.P

S.P

S.B

Nursery

F.B

XXVII. Our route is from the left (lower) to the right on this 1907 extract. The 1879 line from Scalford to John O'Gaunt is from top to bottom. Its bridges are just visible in the next picture. The 'Old Railway' was in use from 1883 to 1887. Centre left is the direct route to Nottingham, which ceased to carry through trains in 1968. Part of it became the Old Dalby Test Track, which was 12 miles long, eventually, and features in our *Kettering to Nottingham* album.

111. The box had 28 levers and functioned from 15th November 1886 until 18th December 1968, when the track on the right was singled. Wagons stand on one of the two exchange sidings on 16th July 1965. The white fence posts appear to be on the 1883 boundary alignment. (R.Humm coll.)

112. No. 31229 passes Melton Junction with a ballast train from Croft Quarry comprising mainly 'Mermaid' and 'Sealion' hopper wagons on 13th April 1984. On the right is the Old Dalby branch. No. 31229 was allocated to March depot at that time; it survived in revenue-earning use until December 1997. The branch continued to serve the Asfordby Business Park and the test track. The former became Melton Commercial Park in 2017. One of the tenants at the Park included Network Rail, who operated its Rail Innovation and Development Centre for the testing of vehicles and infrastructure from the site. (P.D.Shannon)

MELTON MOWBRAY

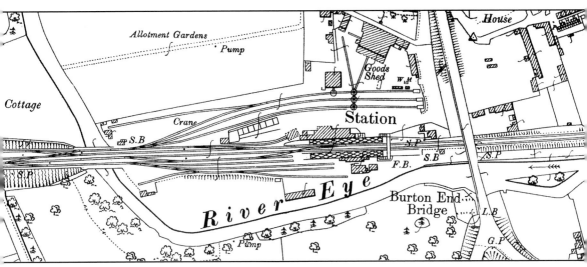

XXVIII. This map is from 1904 and is scaled at 10ins to 1 mile. L.B. refers to a Letter Box and G.P. is a Guide Post. The station was on the new MR main line between London and Scotland from 1880. It was designed to avoid the increasingly busy Leicester area. The Melton Mowbray Gas, Light & Coke Co. had no siding, being founded in 1834. The works carbonised 3247 tons of coal in 1900 and about 10,000 tons in 1950. The company ran its own wagons, and later probably used those of Gas Consolidation Ltd.

113. The station had the suffix 'Town' from 4th November 1954 to 14th June 1965. Initially it was just Melton, but Mowbray was added permanently from 1st November 1866, with 'South' also, from 1923 to 1950, when it became 'Midland' until 1954. This undated postcard features the well-lit water column. The supply would have come direct from the river, initially. The footbridge was erected in 1897. (P.Laming coll.)

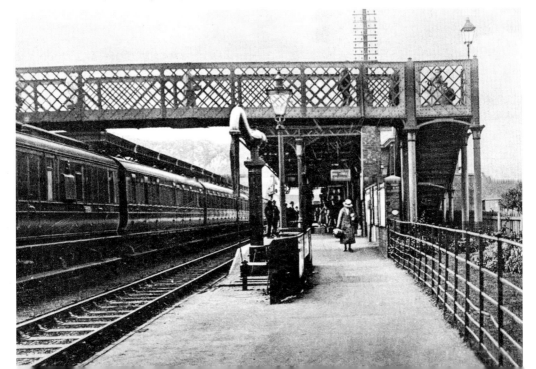

114. This undated view of the south elevation is from the BR era and appears to feature a Humber Hawk (right) and a Morris 10. The gas lamps do not match; we have Sugg's Windsor and Rochester patterns. The portico was added in about 1880 to impress the wealthy. (R.Humm coll.)

115. Within the reflections is the word TOWN, which gives a date range for the photograph. An early report on the fine condition of the first class waiting room was unusual in stating that 'the lavatory seat had a hot water pipe coursing through it'. (R.Humm coll.)

116. The locomotive water tanks offered water at two different pressures. There were water troughs east of the station, fitted for MR expresses in 1905. Seen on 16th July 1965 is class 8F 2-8-0 no. 48381, which was based at Leicester. The yard had a 5-ton capacity crane. (R.Humm coll.)

117. The platforms were limited to four coaches by the time this photograph was taken. The station had an overall roof until April 1876, when it collapsed under a heavy snowfall. There had been a level crossing in the foreground until 1900. Its signal box closed on 9th August 1942. Nos 20161 and 20168 pass through with a solitary brake van in tow on 13th April 1984. By this time very few trains required a brake van. On the far right is a siding belonging to the goods yard, which was out of use at the time of the photograph; it is interesting to note the lack of fencing between the station car park and the goods yard, at that time. (P.D.Shannon)

118. The tall 1942 box had 45 levers and panels came as additions in 1978 and 1986. Melton Mowbray goods yard was used by the pioneering but ultimately unsuccessful Charterail for its pet food traffic in bi-modal 'Piggyback' wagons to Glasgow (Deanside) and London (Cricklewood). This photograph dated 27th August 1991 shows loading in progress. Each wagon had a hinged central section that could be swung out in order for a road trailer to be backed onto it and then moved back into the main body of the wagon and secured for transit. A mobile hydraulic power unit was required to activate the air suspension of the trailers before unloading and a retractable lifting beam held the weight of the trailer while a road tractor unit drew up to it. Although it seemed a good idea at the time, the operation was very labour intensive. Another drawback was that the Charterail curtain-sided trailers were rather smaller than standard road trailers, because they had to fit within the BR loading gauge when loaded onto the wagons. Charterail ceased rail operations in August 1992. No. 08511 waits with loaded wagons on 23rd October 1991. (M.J.Stretton coll.)

For other views of both stations serving the town, see
Kettering to Nottingham **and** *Market Harborough to Newark.*

119. The well-surfaced goods yard was the site of an Open Day on 25th May 1992. Nos 60012, 47345 *Scimitar* and 56078 were stars of the show. All activities would cease within three months. (R.J.Stewart-Smith)

120. The station canopies were reglazed and a new footbridge came in 2011. We see the station on 9th August 2016 with three-car class 170 Turbo unit no. 170109 forming the 10.22 Birmingham to Stansted Airport Cross Country service. The station won a 'highly commended' award at the National Rail Awards in 2014, for Small Station of the Year. It still had part-time staffing in 2016 and around 0.25m passengers per annum. (R.Geach)

MP Middleton Press

EVOLVING THE ULTIMATE RAIL ENCYCLOPEDIA

Easebourne Midhurst GU29 9AZ. Tel:01730 813169

www.middletonpress.co.uk email:info@middletonpress.co.uk
A-978 0 906520 B- 978 1 873793 C- 978 1 901706 D-978 1 904474
E - 978 1 906008 F - 978 1 908174 G - 978 1 910356

All titles listed below were in print at time of publication - please check current availability by looking at our website - *www.middletonpress.co.uk* or by requesting a Brochure which includes our *LATEST* RAILWAY TITLES also our TRAMWAY, TROLLEYBUS, MILITARY and COASTAL series

A
Abergavenny to Merthyr C 91 8
Abertillery & Ebbw Vale Lines D 84 5
Aberystwyth to Carmarthen E 90 1
Allhallows - Branch Line to A 62 8
Alton - Branch Lines to A 11 6
Andover to Southampton A 82 6
Ascot - Branch Lines around A 64 2
Ashburton - Branch Line to B 95 4
Ashford - Steam to Eurostar B 67 1
Ashford to Dover A 48 2
Austrian Narrow Gauge D 04 3
Avonmouth - BL around D 42 5
Aylesbury to Rugby D 91 3

B
Baker Street to Uxbridge D 90 6
Bala to Llandudno E 87 1
Banbury to Birmingham D 27 2
Banbury to Cheltenham E 63 5
Bangor to Holyhead F 01 7
Bangor to Portmadoc E 72 7
Barking to Southend C 80 2
Barmouth to Pwllheli E 53 6
Barry - Branch Lines around D 50 0
Bartlow - Branch Lines to F 27 7
Bath Green Park to Bristol C 36 9
Bath to Evercreech Junction A 60 4
Beamish 40 years on rails E94 9
Bedford to Wellingborough D 31 9
Berwick to Drem F 64 2
Berwick to St. Boswells F 75 8
B'ham to Tamworth & Nuneaton F 63 5
Birkenhead to West Kirby F 61 1
Birmingham to Wolverhampton E253
Blackburn to Hellifield F 95 6
Bletchley to Cambridge D 94 4
Bletchley to Rugby E 07 9
Bodmin - Branch Lines around B 83 1
Boston to Lincoln F 80 2
Bournemouth to Evercreech Jn A 46 8
Bournemouth to Weymouth A 57 4
Bradshaw's History F18 5
Bradshaw's Rail Times 1850 F 13 0
Bradshaw's Rail Times 1895 F 11 6
Branch Lines series - see town names
Brecon to Neath D 43 2
Brecon to Newport D 16 6
Brecon to Newtown E 06 2
Brighton to Eastbourne A 16 1
Brighton to Worthing A 03 1
Bristol to Taunton D 03 6
Bromley South to Rochester B 23 7
Bromsgrove to Birmingham D 87 6
Bromsgrove to Gloucester D 73 9
Broxbourne to Cambridge F16 1
Brunel - A railtour D 74 6
Bude - Branch Line to B 29 9
Burnham to Evercreech Jn B 68 0

C
Cambridge to Ely D 55 5
Canterbury - BLs around B 58 9
Cardiff to Dowlais (Cae Harris) E 47 5
Cardiff to Pontypridd E 95 6
Cardiff to Swansea E 42 0
Carlisle to Hawick E 85 7
Carmarthen to Fishguard E 66 6
Caterham & Tattenham Corner B251
Central & Southern Spain NG E 91 8
Chard and Yeovil - BLs a C 30 7
Charing Cross to Dartford A 75 8
Charing Cross to Orpington A 96 3
Cheddar - Branch Line to B 90 9
Cheltenham to Andover C 43 7
Cheltenham to Redditch D 81 4
Chester to Birkenhead F 21 5
Chester to Manchester F 51 2
Chester to Rhyl E 93 2
Chester to Warrington F 40 6
Chichester to Portsmouth A 14 7
Clacton and Walton - BLs to F 04 8
Clapham Jn to Beckenham Jn B 36 7
Cleobury Mortimer - BLs a E 18 5
Clevedon & Portishead - BLs to D180
Consett to South Shields E 57 4
Cornwall Narrow Gauge D 56 2
Corris and Vale of Rheidol E 65 9
Coventry to Leicester G 00 5
Craven Arms to Llandeilo E 35 2
Craven Arms to Wellington E 33 8
Crawley to Littlehampton A 34 5
Crewe to Manchester F 57 4
Crewe to Wigan G 12 8
Cromer - Branch Lines around C 26 0
Croydon to East Grinstead B 48 0
Crystal Palace & Catford Loop B 87 1
Cyprus Narrow Gauge E 13 0

D
Darjeeling Revisited F 09 3
Darlington Leamside Newcastle E 28 4
Darlington to Newcastle D 98 2
Dartford to Sittingbourne B 34 3
Denbigh - Branch Lines around F 32 1
Derby to Chesterfield G 11 1
Derby to Stoke-on-Trent F 93 2
Derwent Valley - BL to the D 06 7
Devon Narrow Gauge E 09 3
Didcot to Banbury D 02 9
Didcot to Swindon C 84 0
Didcot to Winchester C 13 0
Dorset & Somerset NG D 76 0
Douglas - Laxey - Ramsey E 75 8
Douglas to Peel C 88 8
Douglas to Port Erin C 55 0
Douglas to Ramsey D 39 5
Dover to Ramsgate A 78 9
Drem to Edinburgh G 06 7
Dublin Northwards in 1950s E 31 4
Dunstable - Branch Lines to E 27 7

E
Ealing to Slough C 42 0
Eastbourne to Hastings A 27 7
East Cornwall Mineral Railways D 22 7
East Croydon to Three Bridges A 53 6
Eastern Spain Narrow Gauge E 56 7
East Grinstead - BLs to A 07 9
East Kent Light Railway A 61 1
East London - Branch Lines of C 44 4
East London Line B 80 0
East of Norwich - Branch Lines E 69 7
Effingham Junction - BLs a A 74 1
Ely to Norwich C 90 1
Enfield Town & Palace Gates D 32 6
Epsom to Horsham A 30 7
Eritrean Narrow Gauge E 38 3
Euston to Harrow & Wealdstone C 89 5
Exeter to Barnstaple B 15 2
Exeter to Newton Abbot C 49 9
Exeter to Tavistock B 69 5
Exmouth - Branch Lines to B 00 8

F
Fairford - Branch Line to A 52 9
Falmouth, Helston & St. Ives C 74 1
Fareham to Salisbury A 67 3
Faversham to Dover B 05 3
Felixstowe & Aldeburgh - BL to D 20 3
Fenchurch Street to Barking C 20 8
Festiniog - 50 yrs of enterprise C 83 3
Festiniog 1946-55 E 01 7
Festiniog in the Fifties B 68 8
Festiniog in the Sixties B 91 6
Ffestiniog in Colour 1955-82 F 25 3
Finsbury Park to Alexandra Pal C 02 8
French Metre Gauge Survivors F 88 8
Frome to Bristol B 77 0

G
Galashiels to Edinburgh F 52 9
Gloucester to Bristol D 35 7
Gloucester to Cardiff D 66 1
Gosport - Branch Lines around A 36 9
Greece Narrow Gauge D 72 2

H
Hampshire Narrow Gauge D 36 4
Harrow to Watford D 14 2
Harwich & Hadleigh - BLs to F 02 4
Harz Revisited F 62 8
Hastings to Ashford A 37 6
Hawick to Galashiels F 36 9
Hawkhurst - Branch Line to A 66 6
Hayling - Branch Line to A 12 3
Hay-on-Wye - BL around D 92 0
Haywards Heath to Seaford A 28 4
Hemel Hempstead - BLs to D 88 3
Henley, Windsor & Marlow - BLa C77 2
Hereford to Newport D 54 8
Hertford & Hatfield - BLs a E 58 1
Hertford Loop E 71 0
Hexham to Carlisle D 75 3
Hexham to Hawick F 08 6
Hitchin to Peterborough D 07 4
Holborn Viaduct to Lewisham A 81 9
Horsham - Branch Lines to A 02 4
Huntingdon - Branch Line to A 93 2

I
Ilford to Shenfield C 97 0
Ilfracombe - Branch Line to B 21 3
Industrial Rlys of the South East A 09 3
Ipswich to Diss F 81 9
Ipswich to Saxmundham C 41 3
Isle of Man Railway Journey F 94 9
Isle of Wight Lines - 50 yrs C 12 3
Italy Narrow Gauge F 17 8

K
Kent Narrow Gauge C 45 1
Kettering to Nottingham F 82-6
Kidderminster to Shrewsbury E 10 9
Kingsbridge - Branch Line to C 98 7
Kings Cross to Potters Bar E 62 8
King's Lynn to Hunstanton F 58 1
Kingston & Hounslow Loops A 83 3
Kingswear - Branch Line to C 17 8

L
Lambourn - Branch Line to C 70 3
Launceston & Princetown - BLs C 19 2
Leek - Branch Line From G 01 2
Leicester to Burton F 85 7
Leicester to Nottingham G 15 9
Lewisham to Dartford A 92 5
Lincoln to Cleethorpes F 56 7
Lincoln to Doncaster G 03 6
Lines around Stamford F 98 7
Lines around Wimbledon B 75 6
Liverpool Street to Chingford D 01 2
Liverpool Street to Ilford C 34 5
Llandeilo to Swansea E 46 8
London Bridge to Addiscombe B 20 6
London Bridge to East Croydon A 58 1
Longmoor - Branch Lines to A 41 3
Looe - Branch Line to C 22 2
Loughborough to Nottingham F 68 0
Lowestoft - BLs around E 40 6
Ludlow to Hereford E 14 7
Lydney - Branch Lines around E 26 0
Lyme Regis - Branch Line to A 45 1
Lynton - Branch Line to B 04 6

M
Machynlleth to Barmouth E 54 3
Maesteg and Tondu Lines E 06 2
Majorca & Corsica Narrow Gauge F 41 3
March - Branch Lines around B 09 1
Market Drayton - BLs around F 67 3
Market Harborough to Newark F 86 4
Marylebone to Rickmansworth D 49 4
Melton Constable to Yarmouth Bch E031
Midhurst - Branch Lines of E 78 9
Midhurst - Branch Lines to F 00 0
Minehead - Branch Line to A 80 2
Mitcham Junction Lines B 01 5
Monmouth - Branch Lines to E 20 8
Monmouthshire Eastern Valleys D 71 5
Moretonhampstead - BL to C 27 7
Moreton-in-Marsh to Worcester D 26 5
Morpeth to Bellingham F 87 1
Mountain Ash to Neath D 80 7

N
Newark to Doncaster F 78 9
Newbury to Westbury C 66 6
Newcastle to Hexham D 69 2
Newport (IOW) - Branch Lines to A 26 0
Newquay - Branch Lines to C 71 0
Newton Abbot to Plymouth C 60 4
Newtown to Aberystwyth E 41 3
Northampton to Peterborough F 92 5
North East German NG D 44 9
Northern Alpine Narrow Gauge F 37 6
Northern France Narrow Gauge C 75 8
Northern Spain Narrow Gauge E 83 3
North London Line B 94 7
North of Birmingham F 55 0
North of Grimsby - Branch Lines G 09 8
North Woolwich - BLs around C 65 9
Nottingham to Boston F 70 3
Nottingham to Lincoln F 43 7
Nuneaton to Loughborough G 08 1

O
Ongar - Branch Line to E 05 5
Orpington to Tonbridge B 03 9
Oswestry - Branch Lines around E 60 4
Oswestry to Whitchurch E 81 9
Oxford to Bletchley D 57 9
Oxford to Moreton-in-Marsh D 15 9

P
Paddington to Ealing C 37 6
Paddington to Princes Risborough C819
Padstow - Branch Line to B 54 1
Pembroke and Cardigan - BLs to F 29 1
Peterborough to Kings Lynn E 32 1
Peterborough to Lincoln F 89 5
Peterborough to Newark F 72 7
Plymouth - BLs around B 98 5
Plymouth to St. Austell C 63 5
Pontypool to Mountain Ash D 65 4
Pontypridd to Merthyr F 14 7
Pontypridd to Port Talbot E 86 4
Porthmadog 1954-94 - BLa B 31 2
Portmadoc 1923-46 - BLa B 13 8
Portsmouth to Southampton A 31 4
Portugal Narrow Gauge E 67 3
Potters Bar to Cambridge D 70 8
Preston to Blackpool G 16 6
Princes Risborough - BL to D 05 0
Princes Risborough to Banbury C 85 7

R
Railways to Victory C 16 1
Reading to Basingstoke B 27 5
Reading to Didcot C 79 6
Reading to Guildford A 47 5
Redhill to Ashford A 73 4
Return to Blaenau 1970-82 C 64 2
Rhyl to Bangor F 15 4
Rhymney & New Tredegar Lines E 48 2
Rickmansworth to Aylesbury D 61 6
Romania & Bulgaria NG E 23 9
Romneyrail C 32 1
Ross-on-Wye - BLs around E 30 7
Ruabon to Barmouth E 84 0
Rugby to Birmingham E 37 6
Rugby to Loughborough F 12 3
Rugby to Stafford F 07 9
Rugeley to Stoke-on-Trent F 90 1
Ryde to Ventnor A 19 2

S
Salisbury to Westbury B 39 8
Sardinia and Sicily Narrow Gauge F 50 5
Saxmundham to Yarmouth C 69 7
Saxony & Baltic Germany Revisited F 71 0
Saxony Narrow Gauge D 47 0
Seaton & Sidmouth - BLs to A 95 6
Selsey - Branch Line to A 04 8
Sheerness - Branch Line to B 16 2
Shenfield to Ipswich E 96 3
Shrewsbury - Branch Line to A 86 4
Shrewsbury to Chester E 70 3
Shrewsbury to Crewe F 48 2
Shrewsbury to Ludlow E 21 5
Shrewsbury to Newtown E 29 1
Sierra Leone Narrow Gauge D 28 9
Sirhowy Valley Line E 12 3
Sittingbourne to Ramsgate A 90 1
Skegness & Mablethorpe - BL to F 84 0
Slough to Newbury C 56 7
South African Two-foot gauge E 51 2
Southampton to Bournemouth A 42 0
Southend & Southminster BLs E 76 5
Southern Alpine Narrow Gauge F 22 2
Southern France Narrow Gauge C 47 5
South London Line B 46 6
South Lynn to Norwich City F 03 1
Southwold - Branch Line to A 15 4
Spalding - Branch Lines around E 52 9
Spalding to Grimsby F 65 9 6
Stafford to Chester F 34 5
Stafford to Wellington F 59 8
St Albans to Bedford D 08 1
St. Austell to Penzance C 67 3
St. Boswell to Berwick F 44 4
Steaming Through Isle of Wight A
Steaming Through West Hants A
Stourbridge to Wolverhampton E
St. Pancras to Barking D 68 5
St. Pancras to Folkestone E 88 8
St. Pancras to St. Albans C 78 9
Stratford to Cheshunt F 53 6
Stratford-u-Avon to Birmingham
Stratford-u-Avon to Cheltenham C
Sudbury - Branch Lines to F 19 2
Surrey Narrow Gauge C 87 1
Sussex Narrow Gauge C 68 0
Swaffham - Branch Lines around
Swanage to 1999 - BL to A 33 8
Swanley to Ashford B 45 9
Swansea - Branch Lines around F
Swansea to Carmarthen E 59 8
Swindon to Bristol C 96 3
Swindon to Gloucester D 46 3
Swindon to Newport D 30 2
Swiss Narrow Gauge C 94 9

T
Talyllyn 60 E 98 7
Tamworth to Derby F 76 5
Taunton to Barnstaple B 60 2
Taunton to Exeter C 82 6
Taunton to Minehead F 39 0
Tavistock to Plymouth B 88 6
Tenterden - Branch Line to A 21 5
Three Bridges to Brighton A 35 2
Tilbury Loop C 86 4
Tiverton - BLs around C 62 8
Tivetshall to Beccles D 41 8
Tonbridge to Hastings A 44 4
Torrington - Branch Lines to B 37
Tourist Railways of France G 04 3
Towcester - BLs around E 39 0
Tunbridge Wells BLs A 32 1

U
Upwell - Branch Line to B 64 0
Uttoxeter to Macclesfield G 05 0

V
Victoria to Bromley South A 98 7
Victoria to East Croydon A 40 6
Vivarais Revisited E 08 6

W
Walsall Routes F 45 1
Wantage - Branch Line to D 25 8
Wareham to Swanage 50 yrs D 0
Waterloo to Windsor A 54 3
Waterloo to Woking A 38 3
Watford to Leighton Buzzard D 45
Wellingborough to Leicester F 73
Welshpool to Llanfair E 49 9
Wenford Bridge to Fowey C 09 3
Westbury to Bath B 55 8
Westbury to Taunton C 76 5
West Cornwall Mineral Rlys D 48
West Croydon to Epsom B 08 4
West German Narrow Gauge D 9
West London - BLs of C 50 5
West London Line B 84 8
West Wiltshire - BLs of D 12 8
Weymouth - BLs A 65 9
Willesden Jn to Richmond B 71
Wimbledon to Beckenham C 58
Wimbledon to Epsom B 62 6
Wimborne - BLs around A 97 0
Wirksworth - Branch Lines to G
Wisbech - BLs around C 01 7
Witham & Kelvedon - BLs a E 82
Woking to Alton A 59 8
Woking to Portsmouth A 25 3
Woking to Southampton A 55 0
Wolverhampton to Shrewsbury E
Wolverhampton to Stafford F 79
Worcester to Birmingham D 97 5
Worcester to Hereford D 38 8
Worthing to Chichester A 06 2
Wrexham to New Brighton F 47 5
Wroxham - BLs around F 31 4

Y
Yeovil - 50 yrs change C 38 3
Yeovil to Dorchester A 76 5
Yeovil to Exeter A 91 8
York to Scarborough F 23 9